The Quotable Book Lover

The Quotable Book Lover

EDITED BY
BEN JACOBS AND HELENA HJALMARSSON

FOREWORD BY NICHOLAS A. BASBANES

THE LYONS PRESS

Design by Alexander Graphics Ltd., Plainfield, Indiana
Printed in the United States of America

10 9 8 7 6 5 4 3 2 1

Library of Congress Cataloging-in-Publication Data
The Quotable book lover / edited by Ben Jacobs and Helena Hjalmarsson
 ; foreword by Nicholas Basbanes.
        p.   cm.
    Includes bibliographical references and index.
    ISBN 1-55821-882-3
    1. Books and reading Quotations, maxims, etc.   I. Jacobs, Ben.
II. Hjalmarsson, Helena.
PN6084.B65Q68   1999
808.88'2—dc21   99-21694
                                                             CIP

Contents

Foreword

Nowhere in this rich selection of timeless quotations is there any resonant expression of love for a laptop computer, an operating system, or the myriad kinds of software that permeate the marketplace today with such dismaying abundance.

If it is true, as some people suggest, that a microchip-driven "paradigm shift" has occasioned the imminent death of the printed word, then the extraordinary passion people have lavished on their books through the centuries has entered a dramatic new phase, possibly one that may even presage its demise. Or so we would be led to believe.

Still, books are changing, that is without question, and how they are being produced and marketed is changing just as profoundly. But is the book dead? Are the sentiments expressed in these pages by so many different people, over such a broad expanse of time, about to become charming anachronisms, quaint relics of history, bits of cultural evidence, as John Milton would have it, to be preserved in a vial? Is it possible that libraries will become "book museums," and that the specimens on display under glass will be curious examples of an archaic medium that educated, informed, and enlightened so much of the world for so many hundreds of years?

These are not matters of idle speculation to be pondered casually, at least not for the members of the American Library Association who will be attending a symposium in the year 2000 to debate these very issues. It will be merely the latest in a series of scholarly conferences mounted in recent years to explore various facets of the subject. One gathering in 1994 at the then newly established Center for Semiotic and Cognitive Studies at the University of San Marino in California was aptly called "The Future of the Book." Another, in the spring of 1999 at Brown University in Providence, Rhode Island, called "Technological Platforms for Twenty-first Century Literature," devoted three days to the writing of fiction and poetry on computer—hypertext as an art form—with demonstrations presented by a number of its prominent practitioners. One of the more vexing concerns was expressed by an author who was worried about producing material that ultimately is "unreadable," and by that she did not mean by people who may be literate or illiterate, but by people without the right machinery, the correct software, or the technical dexterity to access her work.

Most ominous of all, perhaps, is the prospect that electronic books may be the only objects people will ever need to read. When plans were being developed in the early 1990s for a new state university to be built on the grounds of an abandoned military base in Monterey, California, no provisions were made at first for a library. Especially disturbing was a report that the exclusion was not an oversight, but part of a "mission" to eliminate formal restraints and to teach vast numbers of students through electronic sources.

When word of the omission reached the press, specifications were abruptly modified. A building with shelves in it was worked into the final layout, and a rudimentary selection of twenty-five thousand books was there to greet the first undergraduates when they arrived on campus. "In this institution, change is at the core," the university president explained unapologetically to a journalist.

And the direction, he emphasized, is clearly plotted. "If you think that technology is the worst thing in the world, then you really shouldn't come here."

In an 1815 letter to John Adams, Thomas Jefferson confessed that he could not live without books. It was a flat-out statement, written on a sheet of paper in pen and ink, expressed simply and in a forthright manner: "I cannot live without books."

Jefferson was a modern man, it must be noted, a thinker of the first magnitude, and a lover of technology who took special pleasure in tinkering with gadgets, as any visitor to his delightful house in Monticello will readily discern. By sending his precious library to Washington, D.C., after the destruction of the capital in the War of 1812, he is the father of the Library of Congress as we know it today. Somehow, it is difficult to imagine him saying, with any degree of intensity, "I cannot live without my computer."

It may well be true, of course, that people of the twenty-first century will be unable to live without computers. Indeed, it may even be the case now. This essay is being written on a word processor, a circumstance that should come as no great surprise to anyone.

What might raise a few eyebrows is the admission that parts of it were dictated into a computer through a program that recognizes my speech patterns, and converts them instantly into words on a screen.

This tool is far from satisfactory—please notice that I said "parts" of the essay were dictated into my computer—but I have no doubt that in five years the deficiencies I find so annoying today will have been worked out, and that I will use the system to transcribe the interviews I now spend hours deciphering myself.

That is progress I will welcome with boundless enthusiasm, because when that happy day arrives I will be able to spend more of my time writing, and less on the thoughtless but necessary exercises that consume so much effort. It is this kind of direction, I think, that awaits the printed book, that after finally being relieved of handling every form of mundanity, it can now concentrate on achieving its full potential as a creative medium.

With the invention of photography in the 1830s, there was widespread anxiety about the certain death of painting as a form of artistic expression. Today, more than a century and a half has gone by, and the world has celebrated the achievements of such giants as Winslow Homer, Claude Monet, Vincent Van Gogh, Mary Cassatt, and Pablo Picasso, and coined phrases like Impressionism, Post-Impressionism, Modernism, Abstract Expressionism, and Post-Modernism to identify the various movements that have explored exciting new directions during that time.

The awe that we feel for the written word is endemic to the species, apparent from the earliest of times, and the conviction that books still matter is evident in the pages that follow. Thankfully, the passion is not about to abandon us just yet.

—Nicholas A. Basbanes
April 1999

Preface

The quotations in this book traveled a wide variety of routes before arriving here. Though most are from our own reading, some are quotes quoted by others, or have been drawn from that vast well of memory we all rely on; still others have come from friends who themselves remembered or collected them from their reading. In a few cases, memory may have been inexact—and sources defied our best efforts to track the words to their origins. In such instances, the quotations were simply too interesting to be left out and we took the bold step of including them herein, with the hope that readers would correct us as need be. Mostly, we wanted to offer a full and engaging group of comments on various aspects of books and writing, a collection that we hope you will enjoy reading as much as we have enjoyed compiling into *The Quotable Book Lover*.

I

In Praise of Books

The books we read help to shape who we are. Reading offers us, as children, our first independence—allowing us to travel far beyond the confines of our immediate world. Books introduce us to great figures in history, narratives that stir our spirit, fictions that tug us out of ourselves and into the lives of a thousand others, and visions of every era through which human beings have lived. And in the process of stretching who we are, books also connect us to all others—of our own or previous times—who have read what we've read. In the community of readers, we instantly become linked to those who share our love for specific characters or passages.

"A well-composed book," says Caroline Gordon, "is a magic carpet on which we are wafted to a world that we cannot enter in any other way."

Here, then, are some words in praise of that magic carpet.

Books may well be the only true magic.

ALICE HOFFMAN

———•·•———

A well-composed book is a magic carpet on which we are wafted to a world that we cannot enter in any other way.

CAROLINE GORDON (1895–1981)

———•·•———

Books are the carriers of civilization . . . They are companions, teachers, magicians, bankers of the treasures of the mind. Books are humanity in print.

BARBARA W. TUCHMAN (1912–1989)

———•·•———

Good books are the warehouses of ideas.

H. G. WELLS (1866–1946)

Books admitted me to their world open-handedly, as people for their most part, did not. The life I lived in books was one of ease and freedom, worldly wisdom, glitter, dash and style.

> JONATHAN RABAN
> *FOR LOVE AND MONEY* (1987)

I grew up kissing books and bread.

> SALMAN RUSHDIE
> *IMAGINARY HOMELANDS* (1992)

Bread and books: food for the body and food for the soul—what could be more worthy of our respect, and even love?

> SALMAN RUSHDIE
> *IMAGINARY HOMELANDS* (1992)

A book is a version of the world. If you do not like it, ignore it; or offer your own version in return.

> SALMAN RUSHDIE
> *IMAGINARY HOMELANDS* (1992)

How beautiful to a genuine lover of reading are the sullied leaves and worn-out appearance, nay the very odour (beyond Russia) if we would not forget kind feelings in fastidiousness, of an old "Circulating library" *Tom Jones* or *Vicar of Wakefield*. How they speak of the thousand thumbs that have turned over their pages with delight.

CHARLES LAMB
"DETACHED THOUGHTS ON BOOKS AND READING" (1822)

A book reads the better which is our own, and has been so long known to us, that we know the topography of its blots, and dog's cars, and can trace the dirt in it to having read it at tea with buttered muffins.

CHARLES LAMB
LAST ESSAYS OF ELIA (1833)

Books must be the axe to break the frozen sea inside me.

FRANZ KAFKA (1883–1924)

A good book is the precious lifeblood of a master spirit, embalmed and treasured up on a purpose to a life beyond life.

> JOHN MILTON
> "AREOPAGITICA" (1644)

———•·•·•———

For books are not absolutely dead things, but do contain a potency of life in them to be as active as that soul whose progeny they are: nay, they do preserve as in a vial the purest effigy and extraction of that living intellect that bred them.

> JOHN MILTON
> "AREOPAGITICA" (1644)

———•·•·•———

An author who speaks about his own books is almost as bad as a mother who talks about her own children.

> BENJAMIN DISRAELI
> A SPEECH IN GLASGOW (NOVEMBER 19, 1873)

A bibliophile of little means is likely to suffer often. Books don't slip from his hands but fly past him through the air, high as birds, high as prices.

PABLO NERUDA (1904–1973)
MEMOIRS (1974)

It is with the reading of books the same as with looking at pictures; one must, without doubt, without hesitations, with assurance, admire what is beautiful.

VINCENT VAN GOGH (1853–1890)

It is with books as with men: a very small number play a great part.

VOLTAIRE (1694–1778)

Books are the true levellers.

WILLIAM ELLERY CHANNING
"SELF-CULTURE" (1838)

My books are water; those of great geniuses are wine. Everybody drinks water.

MARK TWAIN
NOTEBOOK (DECEMBER 11, 1885)

I suggest that the only books that influence us are those for which we are ready, and which have gone a little farther down our particular path than we have yet got ourselves.

E. M. FORSTER
"TWO CHEERS FOR DEMOCRACY" (1951)

Laws die, books never.

EDWARD GEORGE BULWER-LYTTON (1803–1873)

Books are necessary to correct the vices of the polite.

OLIVER GOLDSMITH (C. 1730–1774)

Real education consists in drawing the best out of yourself. What better book can there be than the book of humanity?

MOHANDAS K. GANDHI (1869–1948)

I like a thin book because it will steady a table, a leather volume because it will strop a razor, and a heavy book because it can be thrown at a cat.

MARK TWAIN (1835–1910)

Books will speak plain when counsellors blanch.

FRANCIS BACON
"OF COUNSEL" (1625)

The pale usher—threadbare in coat, heart, body, and brain; I see him now. He was ever dusting his old lexicons and grammars, with a queer handkerchief, mockingly embellished with all the gay flags of all the known nations of the world. He loved to dust his old grammars, it somehow mildly reminded him of his own mortality.

HERMAN MELVILLE
MOBY DICK (1851)

The lessons taught in great books are misleading. The commerce in life is rarely so simple and never so just.

ANITA BROOKNER
NOVELISTS IN INTERVIEW (1985)

Books are the best of things, well used; abused, among the worst. What is the right use? What is the one end which all means go to effect? They are for nothing but to inspire.

RALPH WALDO EMERSON
"THE AMERICAN SCHOLAR" (1837)

The good of a book lies in its being read. A book is made up of signs that speak of other signs, which in their turn speak of things.

UMBERTO ECO
THE NAME OF THE ROSE (1981)

Until it is kindled by a spirit as lovingly alive as the one which gave it birth a book is dead to us. Words divested of their magic are but dead hieroglyphs.

HENRY MILLER
THE BOOKS IN MY LIFE (1951)

It is more of a job to interpret the interpretations than to interpret the things, and there are more books about books than about any other subject: we do nothing but write glosses about each other.

MICHEL DE MONTAIGNE
ESSAYS (1580)

Some books are to be tasted, others to be swallowed, and some are to be chewed and digested.

> FRANCIS BACON
> *ESSAYS* (1625)

———•••———

Of all the inanimate objects, of all men's creations, books are the nearest to us, for they contain our very thought, our ambitions, our indignations, our illusions, our fidelity to truth and our persistent leaning toward error.

> JOSEPH CONRAD
> "NOTES ON LIFE AND LETTERS" (1857–1924)

———•••———

Books, like proverbs, receive their chief value from the stamp and esteem of ages through which they have passed.

> SIR WILLIAM TEMPLE (1628–1699)

———•••———

Books, the children of the brain.

> JONATHAN SWIFT
> *A TALE OF A TUB* (1704)

Books that you may carry to the fire, and hold readily in one hand, are the most useful after all.

> SAMUEL JOHNSON
> IN SIR JOHN HAWKINS, *LIFE OF JOHNSON* (1787)

Your borrowers of books—those mutilators of collections, spoilers of symmetry of shelves, and creators of odd volumes.

> CHARLES LAMB
> "THE TWO RACES OF MEN"
> *ESSAYS OF ELIA* (1823)

Books think for me.

> CHARLES LAMB
> *ESSAYS OF ELIA* (1823)

The true university of these days is a collection of books.

> THOMAS CARLYLE
> "THE HERO AS MAN OF LETTERS"
> *ON HEROES AND HERO WORSHIP* (1841)

Nature and books belong to the eyes that see them.

> RALPH WALDO EMERSON
> "THE POET"
> *ESSAYS: SECOND SERIES* (1844)

All books are divisible into two classes: the books of the hour, and the books of all Time.

> JOHN RUSKIN
> "OF KINGS' TREASURIES"
> *SESAME AND LILIES* (1865)

Books are good enough in their own way, but they are a mightily bloodless substitute for life.

> ROBERT LOUIS STEVENSON
> "AN APOLOGY FOR IDLERS"
> *VIRGINIBUS PUERISQUE* (1881)

Some books are undeservedly forgotten; none are undeservedly remembered.

W. H. AUDEN
"READING"
THE DYER'S HAND (1962)

"What is the use of a book," thought Alice, "without pictures or conversations?"

LEWIS CARROLL
ALICE'S ADVENTURES IN WONDERLAND (1865)

For books are more than books. They are the life, the very heart and core of ages past, the reason why men lived and worked and died, the essence and quintessence of their lives.

AMY LOWELL (1874–1925)

In some respects the better a book is, the less it demands from the binding.

CHARLES LAMB (1775–1834)

I devoured books like a person taking vitamins, afraid that otherwise I would remain this gelatinous narcissist, with no possibility of ever becoming thoughtful, of ever being taken seriously.

ANNE LAMOTT
BIRD BY BIRD (1995)

There are many people—happy people, it usually appears—whose thoughts at Christmas always turn to books. The notion of a Christmas tree with no books under it is repugnant and unnatural to them.

ROBERTSON DAVIES
THE MERRY HEART (1997)

What spectacle can be more edifying or more seasonable, than that of liberty and learning, each leaning on the other for their mutual and surest support.

JAMES MADISON (1751–1836)
"ON THE LIBRARY OF CONGRESS"

What really knocks me out is a book that, when you're all done reading it, you wish the author that wrote it was a terrific friend of yours.

> J. D. SALINGER
> THE CATCHER IN THE RYE (1951)

The love of novels is the preference of sentiment to the senses.

> RALPH WALDO EMERSON (1803–1882)

People think that because a novel's invented it isn't true. Exactly the reverse is the case. Biography and memoirs can never wholly be true, since they cannot include every conceivable circumstance of what happened. The novel can do that.

> ANTHONY POWELL
> IN THE INDEPENDENT (NOVEMBER 25, 1989)

A novel is balanced between a few true impressions and the multitude of false ones that make up most of what we call life.

> SAUL BELLOW
> NOBEL PRIZE ACCEPTANCE SPEECH (1976)

The novel remains for me one of the few forms where we can record man's complexity and the strength and decency of his longings. Where we can describe, step by step, minute by minute, our not altogether unpleasant struggle to put ourselves into a viable and devout relationship to our beloved and mistaken world.

JOHN CHEEVER
NATIONAL BOOK AWARD ACCEPTANCE SPEECH (1958)

Novel, *n.* A short story padded.

AMBROSE BIERCE
THE DEVIL'S DICTIONARY (1911)

A book is like a man—clever and dull, brave and cowardly, beautiful and ugly. For every flowering thought there will be a page like a wet and mangy mongrel.

JOHN STEINBECK
WRITERS AT WORK—FOURTH SERIES (1976)

Magazines all too frequently lead to books, and should be regarded by the prudent as the heavy petting of literature.

FRAN LEBOWITZ
METROPOLITAN LIFE (1978)

It is chiefly through books that we enjoy intercourse with superior minds.

WILLIAM ELLERY CHANNING (1780–1842)

There is a certain kind of child who awakens from a book as from an abyssal sleep, swimming heavily up through layers of consciousness toward a reality that seems less real than the dream-state that has been left behind. I was such a child.

ANNE FADIMAN
EX LIBRIS (1998)

Books were my pass to personal freedom. I learned to read at age three, and soon discovered there was a whole world to conquer that went beyond our farm in Mississippi.

OPRAH WINFREY (1954–   )

There is no such thing as a moral or immoral book. Books are well written, or badly written. That is all.

OSCAR WILDE
THE PICTURE OF DORIAN GRAY (1891)

The age of the book is about gone.

GEORGE STEINER (1929–   )

Comerado, this is no book,
Who touches this touches a man.

WALT WHITMAN
"SO LONG!" (1881)

———•—•—•———

I cannot live without books.

THOMAS JEFFERSON
IN A LETTER TO JOHN ADAMS (JUNE 10, 1815)

2

On Writing

The written word preserves what otherwise might be lost among the impressions that inundate our lives. Thoughts, insights, and perceptions constantly threaten to leave us before we have the opportunity to grasp their meaning. Writing can keep technology-driven, fast-paced, quick-fix, ambiguity-intolerant modern life from overpowering us—and give us something palpable upon which to reflect. Reflection slows matters down. It analyzes what was previously unexamined, and opens doors to different interpretations of what was there all along. Writing, by encouraging reflection, intensifies life.

Mirroring the many dimensions of writing, this section records a variety of different matters: the joy and satisfaction and technique of writing; how writing can heal; and how it can change society. Though they address diverse issues, the quotes that follow clearly share a common desire—to shed light on the mystery and complexity of both the process of writing and the product.

H.H.

The Challenge of Writing

I think there are four great motives for writing . . . (1) Sheer egoism. Desire to seem clever, to be talked about, to be remembered after death, to get your own back on grown-ups who snubbed you in childhood, etc. . . . (2) Aesthetic enthusiasm . . . (3) Historical impulse. Desire . . . to find out true facts and store them up for the use of posterity. (4) Political purpose . . . Desire to push the world in a certain direction, to alter other people's ideas of the kind of society that they should strive after.

GEORGE ORWELL
"WHY I WRITE" (1947)

I write in order to attain that feeling of tension relieved and function achieved, which a cow enjoys on giving milk.

H. L. MENCKEN (1880–1956)

I write because I want more than one life; I insist on a wider selection. It's greed plain and simple. When my characters join the circus, I'm joining the circus. Although I'm happily married, I spent a great deal of time mentally living with incompatible husbands.

ANNE TYLER (1941–   )

One of the most difficult things is the first paragraph. I have spent many months on a first paragraph and once I get it, the rest comes out very easily. In the first paragraph you solve most of the problems with your book. The theme is defined, the style, the tone.

GABRIEL GARCÍA MÁRQUEZ
IN GEORGE PLIMPTON, ED., *THE WRITER'S CHAPBOOK* (1989)

The futility of all prefaces I long ago realized; for the more a writer strives to make his views clear, the more confusion he creates.

JOHANN WOLFGANG VON GOETHE
POETRY AND TRUTH (1811–1833)

The last thing one discovers in composing a work is what to put first.

BLAISE PASCAL
PENSÉES (1670)

A good writer always works at the impossible. There is another kind who pulls in his horizons, drops his mind as one lowers rifle sights.

JOHN STEINBECK
WRITERS AT WORK—FOURTH SERIES (1976)

A writer needs three things, experience, observation, and imagination, any two of which, at times any one of which, can supply the lack of the others.

WILLIAM FAULKNER
WRITERS AT WORK—FIRST SERIES (1958)

It has taken me years of struggle, hard work and research to learn to make one simple gesture, and I know enough about the art of writing to realize that it would take as many years of concentrated effort to write one simple beautiful sentence.

ISADORA DUNCAN (C. 1878–1927)

A phrase is born into the world both good and bad at the same time. The secret lies in a slight, an almost invisible twist. The lever should rest in your hand, getting warm, and you can only turn it once, not twice.

ISAAC BABEL
"GUY DE MAUPASSANT" (1932)

I began to speak of style, of the army of words, of the army in which all kinds of weapons may come into play. No iron can stab the heart with such force as a period put just at the right place.

ISAAC BABEL
"GUY DE MAUPASSANT" (1932)

A book is a mirror: if an ape looks into it an apostle is hardly likely to look out.

GEORG CHRISTOPH LICHTENBERG (1742–1799)
APHORISMS (1764–1799)

A bad book is as much of a labor to write as a good one; it comes as sincerely from the author's soul.

ALDOUS HUXLEY
POINT COUNTER POINT (1928)

The art of writing, like the art of love, runs all the way from a kind of routine hard to distinguish from piling bricks to a kind of frenzy closely related to delirium tremens.

H. L. MENCKEN
MINORITY REPORT (1956)

With each book you write you should lose the admirers you gained with the previous one.

ANDRÉ GIDE (1869–1951)

It's much more important to write than to be written about.

GABRIEL GARCÍA MÁRQUEZ (1928–   )
WRITERS AT WORK—SIXTH SERIES (1984)

It is just as well that it came to an end. The endless cohabitation with these imaginary people had begun to make me not a little nervous.

HENRIK IBSEN (1828–1906)

Don't tell me the moon is shining; show me the glint of light on broken glass.

ANTON CHEKHOV (1860–1904)

Giving birth to a book is always an abominable torture for me, because it cannot answer my imperious need for universality and totality.

ÉMILE ZOLA (1840–1902)

I think I may boast myself to be, with all possible vanity, the most unlearned and uninformed female who ever dared to be an authoress.

JANE AUSTEN (1775–1817)

To write well, express yourself like the common people, but think like a wise man.

ARISTOTLE (384–322 B.C.)

If you are in difficulties with a book, try the element of surprise: attack it at an hour when it isn't expecting it.

H. G. WELLS (1866–1946)

The difference between the *almost*-right word & the *right* word is really a large matter—it's the difference between the lightning bug and the lightning.

MARK TWAIN
IN A LETTER TO GEORGE BAINTON (1888)

I had a large vocabulary and had been reading constantly since childhood, I had taken words and the art of arranging them.

MAYA ANGELOU (1928–)

True literature can exist only where it is created, not by diligent and trustworthy officials, but by madmen, hermits, heretics, dreamers, rebels, and skeptics.

YEVGENY ZAMYATIN (1884–1937)
A SOVIET HERETIC (1970)

A work that aspires, however humbly, to the condition of art should carry its justification in every line.

JOSEPH CONRAD
PREFACE TO *THE NIGGER OF THE NARCISSUS* (1897)

A writer should never write about the extraordinary. That is for the journalist.

JAMES JOYCE (1882–1941)

If there's a book you really want to read but it hasn't been written yet, then you must write it.

TONI MORRISON (1931–   )

A thousand things to be written had I time: had I power. A very little writing uses up my capacity for writing.

VIRGINIA WOOLF
A WRITER'S DIARY (SEPTEMBER 18, 1927)

As an experience, madness is terrific . . . and in its lava I still find most of the things I write about.

VIRGINIA WOOLF
IN A LETTER TO ETHEL SMYTH (JUNE 22, 1930)

Everything that I have written is closely related to something that I have lived through.

HENRIK IBSEN (1828–1906)

People who write fiction, if they had not taken it up, might have become very successful liars.

ERNEST HEMINGWAY (1899–1961)

The pen is the tongue of the mind.

MIGUEL DE CERVANTES (1547–1616)

The great enemy of clear language is insincerity.

GEORGE ORWELL
"POLITICS AND THE ENGLISH LANGUAGE"
SHOOTING AN ELEPHANT (1950)

Good writers are those who keep the language efficient.

Ezra Pound
ABC of Reading (1934)

I have always liked to let things simmer in my mind for a long time before setting them down on paper.

William Somerset Maugham (1874–1965)

When the emperor Domitian was bored he mangled flies with a bodkin. I write a book.

Edward Dahlberg
The Confessions of Edward Dahlberg (1971)

As for writing, at thirty I was still writing, reading; tearing up industriously. I had not published a word (save reviews). I despaired. Perhaps at that age one is really most a writer. Then one cannot write, not for lack of skill, but because the object is too near, too vast. I think perhaps it must recede before one can take a pen to it.

Virginia Woolf (1882–1941)

Each time I write, each time the authentic words break through, I am changed. The older order that I was collapses and dies. I do not know what words will appear on the page. I follow language, I follow the sound of the words, and I am surprised and transformed by what I record.

SUSAN GRIFFIN

If, at the close of business each evening, I myself can understand what I've written, I feel the day hasn't been totally wasted.

S. J. PERELMAN (1904–1979)

Only that which does not teach, which does not cry out, which does not condescend, which does not explain, is irresistible.

W. B. YEATS (1865–1939)

Good writers define reality; bad ones merely restate it. A good writer turns fact into truth; a bad writer will, more often than not, accomplish the opposite.

EDWARD F. ALBEE
IN *THE SATURDAY REVIEW* (MAY 4, 1966)

I'm only allowed to write to the end of the page, which has a paralysing effect . . . I try to paint and embroider, but these arts are so vapid after writing.

VIRGINIA WOOLF
IN A LETTER TO LADY ROBERT CECIL (SEPTEMBER 29, 1915)

A writer is somebody for whom writing is more difficult than it is for other people.

THOMAS MANN (1875–1955)
ESSAYS OF THREE DECADES

The task of an American writer is not to describe the misgivings of a woman taken in adultery as she looks out of a window at the rain but to describe four hundred people under the light reaching for a foul ball. This is ceremony.

JOHN CHEEVER
THE JOURNALS (1963)

Writing is play in the same way that playing the piano is "play," or putting on a theatrical "play" is play. Just because something's fun doesn't mean it isn't serious.

MARGARET ATWOOD (1939–)

My task which I am trying to achieve is, by the power of the written word, to make you hear, to make you feel—it is, before all, to make you *see!* That—and no more: and it is everything! If I succeed, you shall find there according to your deserts: encouragement, consolation, fear, charm—all you demand; and, perhaps, also that glimpse of truth for which you have forgotten to ask.

JOSEPH CONRAD
PREFACE TO *THE NIGGER OF THE NARCISSUS* (1897)

Read over your compositions, and wherever you meet with a passage which you think is particularly fine, strike it out.

SAMUEL JOHNSON (1709–1784)

Memory is the crux of our humanity. Without memory we have no identities. That is really why I am committing an autobiography.

ERICA JONG (1942–   )

Reading maketh a full man, conference a ready man, and writing an exact man.

FRANCIS BACON
"OF STUDIES"
ESSAYS (1625)

The greatest thing in style is to have a command of metaphor.

ARISTOTLE (384–322 B.C.)

Writing in English is the most ingenious torture ever devised for sins committed in previous lives. The English reading public explains the reason why.

> JAMES JOYCE (1882–1941)

All writers are vain, selfish and lazy, and at the very bottom of their motives lies a mystery.

> GEORGE ORWELL
> "WHY I WRITE"
> *COLLECTED ESSAYS* (1968)

Writing taught my father to pay attention; my father in turn taught other people to pay attention and then to write down their thoughts and observations.

> ANNE LAMOTT
> *BIRD BY BIRD* (1995)

Writers, you know, are the beggars of western society.

> OCTAVIO PAZ (1914–1998)
> IN *THE INDEPENDENT* (DECEMBER 30, 1990)

Each writer is born with a repertory company in his head.

GORE VIDAL (1925–   )
IN *DALLAS TIMES HERALD* (JUNE 18, 1978)

In a sense the world dies every time a writer dies, because if he is any good, he has been a wet nurse to humanity during his entire existence and has held earth close around him, like the little obstetrical toad that goes about with a cluster of eggs attached to his legs.

E. B. WHITE
"DOOMSDAY"
THE NEW YORKER (NOVEMBER 17, 1945)

Writing is a socially acceptable form of schizophrenia.

E. L. DOCTOROW
WRITERS AT WORK—SIXTH SERIES (1984)

My own experience has been that the tools I need for my trade are paper, tobacco, food and a little whiskey.

WILLIAM FAULKNER
WRITERS AT WORK—FIRST SERIES (1958)

Writers aren't exactly people . . . they're a whole lot of people trying to be one person.

F. SCOTT FITZGERALD (1896–1940)

Most writers regard the truth as their most valuable possession, and therefore are most economical in its use.

MARK TWAIN (1835–1910)

. . . this business of becoming conscious, of being a writer, is ultimately about asking yourself, as my friend Dale puts it, How alive am I willing to be?

ANNE LAMOTT
BIRD BY BIRD (1995)

To evoke in oneself a feeling one has once experienced and having evoked it in oneself by means of movements, lines, colors, sounds, or forms expressed in words, so to transmit that feeling—this is the activity of art.

LEO TOLSTOY
WHAT IS ART? (1898)

The reason why so few good books are written is that so few people who can write know anything.

WALTER BAGEHOT (1826–1877)

Writing a book is a horrible, exhausting struggle, like a long bout of some painful illness. One would never undertake such a thing if one were not driven on by some demon whom one can neither resist nor understand.

> GEORGE ORWELL
> "WHY I WRITE"
> *COLLECTED ESSAYS* (1968)

You don't say, 'I've done it!' You come, with a kind of horrible desperation, to realize that this will do.

> ANTHONY BURGESS
> IN CLARE BOYLAN, ED., *THE AGONY AND THE EGO* (1993)

Everyone thinks writers must know more about the inside of the human head, but that is wrong. They know less, that's why they write. Trying to find out what everyone else takes for granted.

> MARGARET ATWOOD
> *DANCING GIRLS AND OTHER STORIES* (1982)

It took me fifteen years to discover that I had no talent for writing,
but I couldn't give it up because by that time I was too famous.

> ROBERT BENCHLEY (1889–1945)

———

Many remarkable writers not only survive immense amounts of
hack work, they gain know-how from it.

> CHRISTOPHER ISHERWOOD
> *WRITERS AT WORK*—FOURTH SERIES (1976)

———

Often I think writing is a sheer paring away of oneself, leaving
always something thinner, barer, more meagre.

> F. SCOTT FITZGERALD
> IN A LETTER TO HIS DAUGHTER, SCOTTIE (APRIL 27, 1940)

———

True ease in writing comes from art, not chance,
As those move easiest who have learn'd to dance.

> ALEXANDER POPE
> *AN ESSAY ON CRITICISM* (1711)

I write the way women have babies. You don't know it's going to be like that. If you did, there's no way you would go through with it.

TONI MORRISON (1931–   )

If a writer is honest, if what is at stake for him can seem to matter to his readers, then his work may be read. But a writer will work anyway, as I do, as I have, in part to explore this terra incognita, this dangerous ground I seem to need to risk.

FREDERICK BUSCH
A DANGEROUS PROFESSION (1998)

We write to taste life twice, in the moment, and in retrospection . . . We write to be able to transcend our life, to reach beyond it. We write to teach ourselves to speak with others, to record the journey into the labyrinth.

ANAÏS NIN (1903–1977)

Planning to write is not writing. Outlining . . . researching . . . talking to people about what you're doing, none of that is writing. Writing is writing.

E. L. DOCTOROW (1931–   )

In youth men are apt to write more wisely than they really know or feel; and the remainder of life may be not idly spent in realizing and convincing themselves of the wisdom which they uttered long ago.

NATHANIEL HAWTHORNE
PREFACE TO *THE SNOW IMAGE* (1852)

Writing is easy. All you have to do is sit at a typewriter and open a vein.

ATTRIBUTED TO RED (WALTER WELLESLEY) SMITH (1905–1982)

I am an obsessive rewriter, doing one draft and then another and another, usually five. In a way, I have nothing to say but a great deal to add.

GORE VIDAL (1925–   )

I have nothing better to do with my life than to write a book and perhaps nothing worse. Besides, it is a delusion to believe that one has a choice.

EDWARD DAHLBERG
BECAUSE I WAS FLESH (1964)

In written speech, as tone of voice and knowledge of subject are excluded, we are obliged to use many more words, and to use them more exactly. Written speech is the most elaborate form of speech.

LEV VYGOTSKY (1896–1934)
THOUGHT AND LANGUAGE (1986)

I never think at all when I write. Nobody can do two things at the same time and do them both well.

DON MARQUIS (1878–1937)

A book of mine is always a matter of fate. There is something unpredictable about the process of writing, and I cannot prescribe for myself any predetermined course.

C. G. JUNG
MEMORIES, DREAMS, REFLECTIONS (1961)

Oh yes, between fifty and sixty I think I shall write out some very singular books if I live.

VIRGINIA WOOLF (1882–1941)

Don't ask a writer what he's working on. It's like asking someone with cancer about the progress of his disease.

JAY MCINERNEY
BRIGHTNESS FALLS (1992)

I was brought up in the great tradition of the late nineteenth century: that a writer never complains, never explains and never disdains.

JAMES MICHENER
IN *THE OBSERVER* (NOVEMBER 26, 1989)

The shelf life of the modern hardback writer is somewhere between the milk and the yoghurt.

JOHN MORTIMER (1923–   )

I'm the kind of writer that people think other people are reading.

V. S. NAIPAUL
IN *RADIO TIMES* (MARCH 14, 1979)

The problem with patches of purple prose is not that they are purple but that they are patches.

VIRGINIA WOOLF (1882–1941)

Ultimately, literature is nothing but carpentry. With both you are working with reality, a material just as hard as wood.

GABRIEL GARCÍA MÁRQUEZ
WRITERS AT WORK—SIXTH SERIES (1984)

Writing books is the closest men ever come to childbearing.

NORMAN MAILER (1923–)
"MR. MAILER INTERVIEWS HIMSELF"
NEW YORK TIMES BOOK REVIEW (SEPTEMBER 17, 1965)

Style and Structure are the essence of a book; great ideas are hogwash.

VLADIMIR NABOKOV
WRITERS AT WORK—FOURTH SERIES (1976)

Books choose their authors; the act of creation is not entirely a rational and conscious one.

SALMAN RUSHDIE (1947–)
IN *THE INDEPENDENT* (FEBRUARY 4, 1990)

The discipline of the written word punishes both stupidity and dishonesty.

JOHN STEINBECK (1902–1968)
WRITERS AT WORK—FOURTH SERIES (1977)

Writers are people who write books not because they are poor, but because they are dissatisfied with the books which they could buy but do not like.

WALTER BENJAMIN (1892–1940)

Every writer hopes or boldly assumes that his life is in some sense exemplary, that the particular will turn out to be universal.

MARTIN AMIS (1949–)
IN *THE OBSERVER* (AUGUST 30, 1987)

I think of an author as somebody who goes into the marketplace and puts down his rug and says "I will tell you a story," and then he passes the hat.

ROBERTSON DAVIES
THE ENTHUSIASMS OF ROBERTSON DAVIES (1979)

Writers are always selling someone out.

JOAN DIDION
PREFACE TO *SLOUCHING TOWARDS BETHLEHEM* (1968)

The most essential gift for a writer is a built-in, shock-proof, shit detector. This is the writer's radar and all great writers have had it.

ERNEST HEMINGWAY
WRITERS AT WORK—SECOND SERIES (1963)

When a writer becomes the center of his attention, he has become a nudnick, and a nudnick who believes he is profound is even worse than just a plain nudnick.

ISAAC BASHEVIS SINGER (1904–1991)
IN *THE NEW YORK TIMES* (NOVEMBER 26, 1978)

My schedule is flexible, but I am rather particular about my instruments: lined Bristol cards and well-sharpened, not too hard, pencils capped with erasers.

VLADIMIR NABOKOV
WRITERS AT WORK—FOURTH SERIES (1976)

Recently, I observed to a passing tape recorder that I was once a famous novelist. When assured, politely, that I was still known and read, I explained myself. I was speaking, I said, not of me but of a category to which I once belonged that no longer exists. I am still here, but my category is not. To speak today of a famous novelist is like speaking of a famous cabinetmaker, or speedboat designer.

GORE VIDAL
SCREENING HISTORY (1992)

But who shall be the master, the writer or the reader?

DENIS DIDEROT
JACQUES LE FATALISTE (1796)

[The way to write is for as] long as you can live and there is pencil and paper or ink or any machine to do it with, or anything you care to write about, and you feel a fool, and you are a fool, to do it in any other way.

ERNEST HEMINGWAY
GREEN HILLS OF AFRICA (1935)

Writing to Heal

Words are healers of the sick tempered.

> AESCHYLUS (525–456 B.C.)
> *PROMETHEUS BOUND*

For me, writing something down is the only road out.

> ANNE TYLER (1941–   )

It has become a necessity for me to write down my early memories. If I neglect to do so for a single day, unpleasant physical symptoms immediately follow. As soon as I set to work they vanish and my head feels perfectly clear.

> C. G. JUNG
> *MEMORIES, DREAMS, REFLECTIONS* (1961)

[Writing] is a kind of pain I can't do without.

> ROBERT PENN WARREN (1905–1989)

One sheds one's sickness in books—repeats and presents again one's emotions, to be master of them.

D. H. LAWRENCE (1885–1930)

I had written those pages without a specific recipient in mind. For me, those were things I had inside, that occupied me and that I had to expel: tell them, indeed shout them from the roof-tops.

PRIMO LEVI
THE DROWNED AND THE SAVED (1988)

He wrote in order to clarify his thinking and stave off occasional periods of depression, anxiety, and fears of senility. Above all, in the writings he organized his conception of himself and the meaning of his life.

BARBARA MYERHOFF
NUMBER OUR DAYS (1978)

Throughout his writings, Jacob repeatedly could be seen making bearable his periods of anguish and confusion by finding them explicable.

> BARBARA MYERHOFF
> *NUMBER OUR DAYS* (1978)

One can bear anything of which one is able to conceive.

> SUSANNE K. LANGER (1895–1985)

I noted in my intermittent diary: "Life has precisely the value one puts on it," undoubtedly a banal way of putting things but, to me, such insight was so breathlessly new I could not implement it.

> INGMAR BERGMAN
> *THE MAGIC LANTERN* (1988)

I soothe my conscience now with the thought that it is better for hard words to be on paper than that Mummy should carry them in her heart.

> ANNE FRANK (1929–1945)
> *THE DIARY OF A YOUNG GIRL* (1958)

AND ME? I have a burned-down, destroyed country, a demolished town, friends—refugees all over the world . . . But, luckily, I have you Mimmy, and your lined pages, which are always silent, patiently waiting for me to fill them with my sad thoughts.

ZLATA FILIPOVIÂC
ZLATA'S DIARY (1994)

Writing to Change

All my writings may be considered tasks imposed from within; their source was a fateful compulsion. What I wrote were things that assailed me from within myself. I permitted the spirit that moved me to speak out. I have never counted upon any strong response, any powerful resonance, to my writings. They represent a compensation for our times, and I have been impelled to say what no one wants to hear.

> C. G. JUNG
> *MEMORIES, DREAMS, REFLECTIONS* (1961)

It is the writer's privilege to help man endure by lifting his heart, by reminding him of the courage and honor and hope and pride and compassion and pity and sacrifice which has been the glory of his past.

> WILLIAM FAULKNER (1897–1962)

For me the novel is a social vehicle. It reflects society.

MARGARET ATWOOD (1939–)

The pen is mightier than the sword.

EDWARD GEORGE BULWER-LYTTON
RICHELIEU (1839)

In all my work what I try to say is that as human beings we are more alike than we are unalike.

MAYA ANGELOU
INTERVIEW IN *THE NEW YORK TIMES* (JANUARY 20, 1993)

The writer in Western civilization has become not a voice of his tribe, but of his individuality. This is a very narrow-minded situation.

AHARON APPELFELD (1932–)

Nothing I wrote in the thirties saved one Jew from Auschwitz.

ATTRIBUTED TO W. H. AUDEN (1907–1973)

———•·•·•———

At bottom it is always a writer's tendency, his "purpose," his "message," that makes him liked or disliked. The proof of this is the extreme difficulty of seeing any literary merit in a book that seriously damages your deepest beliefs.

GEORGE ORWELL
INSIDE THE WHALE (1940)

———•·•·•———

Hemingway was proud that his books were so close to the earth and yet reached so high in the heaven of art. But when Bernard pronounces the word "journalist" to himself . . . he is not thinking of Hemingway, and the literary form in which he longs to excel is not reportage. Rather, he dreams of publishing editorials in some influential weekly that would make his father's colleagues tremble.

MILAN KUNDERA
IMMORTALITY (1991)

What literature can and should do is change the people who teach the people who don't read the books.

A. S. BYATT
INTERVIEW IN *NEWSWEEK* (JUNE 5, 1995)

When the soul of a man is born in this country, there are nets flung at it to hold it back from flight. You talk to me of nationality, language, religion. I shall try to fly by those nets.

JAMES JOYCE
A PORTRAIT OF THE ARTIST AS A YOUNG MAN (1916)

Books are, in one sense, the basis of all social progress.

KARL MARX (1818–1883)

Artists are the antennae of the race.

EZRA POUND
ABC OF READING (1934)

3

Autobiography and Biography

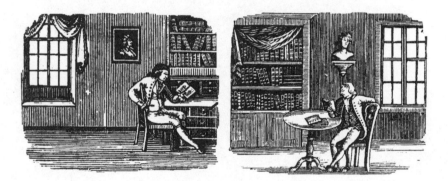

Writing about one's own or another's life poses serious challenges. A writer trying to represent his life in a book engages himself in ongoing negotiation about what information to include and what to withhold, what he believes is true and what he wants readers to think is true. The need for synthesis—coherence, connections between past and present—is a constant struggle for the autobiographical writer. Often, the sense of life as a logical, purposeful unfolding becomes more important to the autobiographer than objective truth. Also vital to writers of autobiographies is the drive to make their work relevant and accessible to their readership—as well as a desire for connection, a social and spiritual need to "reincarnate," to have their hard-won perspective exist outside themselves.

As these quotes attest, autobiographical writing often bears powerful witness to the author's need for self-exploration—the investigation of essential details that illuminate and confirm the direction his life has taken.

Biographical writing, as many of the quotations illustrate, struggles with the difficulty of understanding and explaining another human being's life. Many of the authors quoted here express reservations about a genre that usually pays more attention to the person portrayed than to the person's work. Perhaps this isn't the best approach. Maybe the biography—in contrast to the case history introduced by Freud or the life history inspired by anthropology—does more justice to its subject when it centers on how that person's life and work relate to society as a whole.

Some comments reveal a lack of faith in the fruitfulness of this form, no matter how meticulously researched the subject. And whose life really *is* the subject of a biography—that of the person portrayed, or that of the author?

In attempting to balance objective facts with subjective interpretation, biographers must constantly test the reliability of their sources. And they must always consider the ethical dilemmas that inevitably arise when tempering explicitness with respect for the subject's privacy. These are the issues that make biographical writing especially challenging, interesting, and—as we have found—worthy of comment.

H.H.

Autobiography

Autobiography begins with a sense of being alone. It is an orphan form.

JOHN BERGER
KEEPING A RENDEZVOUS (1991)

I should not talk so much about myself if there were anybody else whom I knew as well. Unfortunately, I am confined to this theme by the narrowness of my experience.

HENRY DAVID THOREAU
WALDEN (1854)

I write fiction and I'm told it's autobiography, I write autobiography and I'm told it's fiction, so since I'm so dim and they're so smart, let *them* decide what it is or isn't.

PHILIP ROTH
DECEPTION (1990)

An autobiography is an obituary in serial form with the last installment missing.

QUENTIN CRISP
THE NAKED CIVIL SERVANT (1968)

Every autobiography . . . becomes an absorbing work of fiction, with something of the charm of a cryptogram.

H. L. MENCKEN
MINORITY REPORT (1956)

So welcome to my life. I hope that what you'll read here will have some meaning. I want it to, as much as I've ever wanted anything.

EARVIN ("MAGIC") JOHNSON JR.
MY LIFE (1992)

When you put down the good things you ought to have done, and leave out the bad things you did do—that's a memoir.

WILL ROGERS (1879–1935)

A well-written Life is almost as rare as a well-spent one.

THOMAS CARLYLE
"JEAN PAUL FRIEDRICH RICHTER"
CRITICAL AND MISCELLANEOUS ESSAYS (1839–1857)

The trouble with writing a book about yourself is that you can't fool. If you write about someone else, you can stretch the truth from here to Finland. If you write about yourself the slightest deviation makes you realize instantly that there may be honor among thieves, but you are just a dirty liar.

GROUCHO MARX
GROUCHO AND ME (1959)

All those writers who write about their childhood! Gentle God, if I wrote about mine you wouldn't sit in the same room as me.

> DOROTHY PARKER
> *WRITERS AT WORK*—FIRST SERIES (1958)

When writing of oneself one should show no mercy. Yet why at the first attempt to discover one's own truth does all inner strength seem to melt away in floods of self-pity and tenderness and rising tears?

> GEORGES BERNANOS
> *THE DIARY OF A COUNTRY PRIEST* (1936)

But there are other things which a man is afraid to tell even to himself, and every decent man has a number of such things stored away in his mind . . . A man's true autobiography is almost an impossibility . . . man is bound to lie about himself.

> FYODOR DOSTOYEVSKY
> "NOTES FROM THE UNDERGROUND" (1864)

There ain't nothing that breaks up homes, country, and nations like somebody publishing their memoirs.

WILL ROGERS (1879–1935)

All autobiographies are lies. I do not mean unconscious, unintentional lies: I mean deliberate lies. No man is bad enough to tell the truth about himself during his lifetime . . . And no man is good enough to tell the truth to posterity in a document which he suppresses until there is nobody left alive to contradict him.

GEORGE BERNARD SHAW
SIXTEEN SELF-SKETCHES (1896)

If you do not want to explore an egoism you should not read autobiography.

H. G. WELLS
EXPERIMENT IN AUTOBIOGRAPHY (1934)

To write one's memoirs is to speak ill of everybody except oneself.

HENRI PHILIPPE PÉTAIN
IN *THE OBSERVER* (MAY 26, 1946)

Autobiography is an unrivaled vehicle for telling the truth about other people.

THOMAS CARLYLE (1795–1881)

There's no such thing as autobiography. There's only art and lies.

JEANETTE WINTERSON
IN *THE GUARDIAN* (JULY 5, 1994)

Biography

Why does writing make us chase the writer? Why can't we leave well enough alone? Why aren't the books enough?

JULIAN BARNES
FLAUBERT'S PARROT (1984)

I am commencing an undertaking, hitherto without precedent, and which will never find an imitator. I desire to set before my fellows the likeness of a man in all the truth of nature, and that man myself.

JEAN JACQUES ROUSSEAU
CONFESSIONS (1781–1788)

I am opposed to writing about the private lives of living authors and psychoanalyzing them while they are alive. Criticism is getting all mixed up with a combination of the junior-FBI-men, discards from Freud and Jung and a sort of columnist peep-hole and missing laundry-list school . . . Every young English professor sees gold in them there sheets now. Imagine what they can do with the soiled sheets of four legal beds by the same writer and you can see why their tongues are slavering.

ERNEST HEMINGWAY
SELECTED LETTERS, 1917–1961 (1981)

A biography is like a handshake down the years, that can become an arm-wrestle.

RICHARD HOLMES
IN *THE TIMES* (LONDON) (OCTOBER 21, 1990)

Biographies generally are a disease of English literature.

GEORGE ELIOT
IN A LETTER TO MRS. THOMAS ADOLPHUS TROLLOPE
(DECEMBER 19, 1879)

Biography is: a system in which the contradictions of a human life are unified.

JOSÉ ORTEGA Y GASSET
THE DEHUMANIZATION OF ART (1948)

Just how difficult it is to write biography can be reckoned by anybody who sits down and considers just how many people know the real truth about his or her love affairs.

REBECCA WEST
IN *VOGUE* (NOVEMBER 1, 1952)

Anyone turning biographer commits himself to lies, to concealment, to hypocrisy, to flattery, and even to hiding his own lack of understanding, for biographical truth is not to be had, and even if it were it couldn't be used.

SIGMUND FREUD
IN A LETTER TO ARNOLD ZWEIG
IN PAUL ROAZEN, *FREUD AND HIS FOLLOWERS* (1971)

How far we are going to read a poet when we can read about a poet is a problem to lay before biographers.

VIRGINIA WOOLF
THE COMMON READER (1932)

Biography is a form by which little people take revenge on big people.

EDMUND WHITE
ON BBC2 PROGRAM *BOOKMARK* (MARCH 9, 1996)

All biography is ultimately fiction.

BERNARD MALAMUD
DUBIN'S LIVES (1979)

Biographers know nothing about the intimate sex lives of their own wives, but they think they know all about Stendhal's or Faulkner's.

MILAN KUNDERA
TESTAMENTS BETRAYED (1995)

Nobody can write the life of a man, but those who have eat and drunk and lived in social intercourse with him.

SAMUEL JOHNSON
IN JAMES BOSWELL, *LIFE OF SAMUEL JOHNSON* (1791)

Biography should be written by an acute enemy.

ARTHUR JAMES BALFOUR (1848–1930)

Every great man nowadays has his disciples, and it is always Judas who writes the biography.

OSCAR WILDE
"THE CRITIC AS ARTIST" (1891)

Biographers are but the clothes and buttons of the man—the biography of the man himself cannot be written.

MARK TWAIN (1835–1910)
AUTOBIOGRAPHY (1924)

How inexpressibly comfortable to know our fellow-creature; to see into him, understand his goings-forth, decipher the whole heart of his mystery: nay, not only to see into him, but even to see out of him, to view the world altogether as he views it.

THOMAS CARLYLE (1795–1881)

There has rarely passed a life of which a judicious and faithful narrative would not be useful.

SAMUEL JOHNSON
"DIGNITY AND USES OF BIOGRAPHY" (1750)

There are two classes of authors: the one write the history of their times, the other their biography.

HENRY DAVID THOREAU
JOURNAL (APRIL 22, 1841)

Biography broadens the vision and allows us to live a thousand lives in one.

ELBERT HUBBARD (1856–1915)
THE NOTEBOOK (1927)

4

Reading

Through the eyes of the writer, readers examine life—history, the present, and the future. The best writers let us see through binoculars that magnify and enrich experience; they allow us to see with broader, deeper insight. Through the careful choice of books, through the vision of writers that we trust, we as readers can better understand our own lives as well as the lives of others.

Reading can also help us understand our hardships, build our aspirations, live in someone else's shoes, learn to make a knot or plant a garden or construct a sentence. By building a broader context around our thinking—one that allows absolute answers and beliefs to give way to a much subtler understanding of life's mysteries—reading becomes an essential life tool, a dynamic process that continues to engage and challenge us.

H.H.

How many a man has dated a new era in his life from the reading of a book.

> HENRY DAVID THOREAU
> "READING"
> *WALDEN* (1854)

When we read a story, we inhabit it.

> JOHN BERGER
> *KEEPING A RENDEZVOUS* (1991)

The failure to read good books both enfeebles the vision and strengthens our most fatal tendency—the belief that here and now is all there is.

> ALLAN BLOOM
> *THE CLOSING OF THE AMERICAN MIND* (1987)

The unread story is not a story; it is little black marks on wood pulp. The reader, reading it, makes it live: a live thing, a story.

> URSULA K. LE GUIN
> *DANCING AT THE EDGE OF THE WORLD* (1989)

Until I feared I would lose it, I never loved to read.

> HARPER LEE
> *TO KILL A MOCKINGBIRD* (1960)

With one day's reading, a man may have the key in his hands.

> EZRA POUND
> *THE PISAN CANTOS* (1948)

I always begin at the left with the opening word of the sentence and read towards the right and I recommend this method.

> JAMES THURBER (1894–1961)
> *NEW YORK TIMES BOOK REVIEW* (DECEMBER 4, 1988)

There are two motives for reading a book: one, that you enjoy it; the other, that you can boast about it.

BERTRAND RUSSELL
THE CONQUEST OF HAPPINESS (1930)

The proper study of mankind is books.

ALDOUS HUXLEY
CROME YELLOW (1921)

Let us read and let us dance—two amusements that will never do any harm to the world.

VOLTAIRE (1694–1778)

Most commonly we come to books with blurred and divided minds, asking of fiction that it shall be true, of poetry that it shall be false, of biography that it shall be flattering, of history that it shall enforce our own prejudices . . . Do not dictate to your author; try to become him.

VIRGINIA WOOLF
THE COMMON READER (1932)

I read a book that impresses me, I have to take myself firmly in hand before I mix with other people, otherwise they would think my mind rather queer.

ANNE FRANK (1929–1945)
THE DIARY OF A YOUNG GIRL (1958)

. . . his mind was fallow. It had lain fallow all his life so far as the abstract thought of the books was concerned, and it was ripe for the sowing. It had never been jaded by study, and it bit hold of the knowledge in the books with sharp teeth that would not let go.

JACK LONDON
MARTIN EDEN (1909)

It is a good thing for an uneducated man to read books of quotations.

WINSTON CHURCHILL
ROVING COMMISSION: MY EARLY LIFE (1930)

There are two kinds of books: those that no one reads and those that no one ought to read.

H. L. MENCKEN (1880–1956)

Everyone, in fact, merely reads himself out of a book; and, if he is a forceful personality, he reads himself into it.

JOHANN WOLFGANG VON GOETHE (1749–1832)

The man who reads nothing at all is better educated than the man who reads nothing but newspapers.

THOMAS JEFFERSON (1743–1826)

The many books he read but served to whet his unrest. Every page of every book was a peep-hole into the realm of knowledge. His hunger fed upon what he read, and increased.

JACK LONDON
MARTIN EDEN (1909)

Read not to contradict and confute, nor to believe and take for granted, nor to find talk and discourse; but to weigh and consider.

FRANCIS BACON
"OF STUDIES"
ESSAYS (1625)

Reading furnishes the mind only with materials of knowledge; it is thinking that makes what we read ours.

JOHN LOCKE (1632–1704)

He that loves reading, has everything within his reach. He has but to desire, and he may possess himself of every species of wisdom to judge and power to perform.

WILLIAM GODWIN (1756–1836)

All the glory of the world would be buried in oblivion, unless God had provided mortals with the remedy of books.

BISHOP RICHARD DE BURY (1281–1345)

To be well informed, one must read quickly a great number of merely instructive books. To be cultivated, one must read slowly and with a lingering appreciation the comparatively few books that have been written by men who lived, thought, and felt with style.

ALDOUS HUXLEY (1894–1963)

There is then creative reading as well as creative writing. When the mind is braced by labor and invention, the page of whatever book we read becomes luminous with manifold allusion.

RALPH WALDO EMERSON
"THE AMERICAN SCHOLAR" (1837)

Literature is my Utopia. Here I am not disenfranchised. No barrier of the senses shuts me out from the sweet, gracious discourse of my book friends. They talk to me without embarrassment or awkwardness.

HELEN KELLER
THE STORY OF MY LIFE (1902)

The reading of all good books is like conversation with the finest men of past centuries.

RENÉ DESCARTES
DISCOURSE ON METHOD (1639)

I started reading. I read everything I could get my hands on . . . By the time I was thirteen I had read myself out of Harlem. I had read every book in two libraries and had a card for the Forty-Second Street branch.

JAMES BALDWIN (1924–1987)

Reading makes immigrants of us all—it takes us away from home, but more important, it finds homes for us everywhere.

HAZEL ROCHMAN

All good books are alike in that they are truer than if they had really happened and after you are finished reading one you will feel that all that happened to you and afterwards it all belongs to you: the good and the bad, the ecstasy, the remorse and sorrow, the people and the places and how the weather was. If you can get so that you can give that to people, then you are a writer.

ERNEST HEMINGWAY
"OLD NEWSMAN WRITES"
IN *ESQUIRE* (DECEMBER 1934)

I came to appreciate what good books really were and realized how much I needed them and they gradually gave me a stoical confidence in myself: I was not alone in this world and I would not perish!

MAXIM GORKY (1868–1936)

Keep reading books, but remember that a book's only a book, and you should learn to think for yourself.

MAXIM GORKY (1868–1936)

Language is the soul of intellect, and reading is the essential process by which that intellect is cultivated beyond the commonplace experiences of everyday life.

CHARLES SCRIBNER (1821–1871)

A man, any man, will go considerably out of his way to pick up a silver dollar, but here are golden words, which the wisest men of antiquity have uttered, and whose worth the wise of every succeeding age have assured us of;—and yet we learn to read only as far as Easy Reading . . . a very low level, worthy only of pigmies and manikins.

HENRY DAVID THOREAU
"READING"
WALDEN (1854)

From your parents you learn love and laughter and how to put one foot before the other. But when books are opened you discover that you have wings.

HELEN HAYES (1900–1993)

Ideology wants to convince you that its truth is absolute. A novel shows you that everything is relative.

MILAN KUNDERA (1929–)

Authors have established it as a kind of rule, that a man ought to be dull sometimes; as the most severe reader makes allowances for many rests and nodding places in a voluminous writer.

JOSEPH ADDISON
IN *THE SPECTATOR* (JULY 23, 1711)

I never desire to converse with a man who has written more than he has read.

SAMUEL JOHNSON (1709–1784)

I opened Shakespeare at the age of nine and was electrified. I crept closer and closer to language for protection. I hoarded words like money . . . I depended on language to save me. And after many years of sorrow and illness, it did.

MELISSA GREEN
COLOR IS THE SUFFERING OF LIGHT (1995)

Reading made Don Quixote a gentleman, but believing what he read made him mad.

GEORGE BERNARD SHAW (1856–1950)

Books must be read as deliberately and reservedly as they were written.

HENRY DAVID THOREAU
"READING"
WALDEN (1854)

Read no history: nothing but biography, for that is life without theory.

G. K. CHESTERTON (1874–1936)

This, then, is one of the ways in which we can read these lives and letters; we can watch the famous dead in their familiar habits and fancy sometimes that we are very close and can surmise their secrets . . . But also we can read such books with another aim, not to throw light on literature, not to become familiar with famous people, but to refresh and exercise our own creative powers. Is there not an open window on the right hand of the bookcase?

VIRGINIA WOOLF (1882–1941)
THE COMMON READER (1932)

Books go out into the world, travel mysteriously from hand to hand, and somehow find their way to the people who need them at the time when they need them . . . Cosmic forces guide such passings-along.

ERICA JONG (1942–   )

I took a speed reading course and read *War and Peace* in twenty minutes. It's about Russia.

WOODY ALLEN (1935–   )

To read well—that is, to read true books in a true spirit—is a noble exercise, and one that will task the reader more than any exercise which the customs of the day esteem. It requires a training such as the athletes underwent, the steady intention almost of the whole life to this object.

HENRY DAVID THOREAU
"READING"
WALDEN (1854)

I had read *A Tale of Two Cities* and found it up to my standards as a romantic novel. She opened the first page and I heard poetry for the first time in my life.

Maya Angelou
I Know Why the Caged Bird Sings (1970)

To be allowed, no, invited, into the private lives of strangers, and to share their joys and fears, was a chance to exchange the Southern bitter worm-wood for a cup of mead with *Beowulf* or a hot cup of tea and milk with *Oliver Twist*.

Maya Angelou
I Know Why the Caged Bird Sings (1970)

All I cared about was that she had made tea cookies for me and read to me from her favorite book. It was enough to prove that she liked me.

MAYA ANGELOU

I KNOW WHY THE CAGED BIRD SINGS (1970)

I find television very educational. Every time someone turns it on, I go in the other room and read a book.

GROUCHO MARX (1895–1977)

Writers should be read, but neither seen nor heard.

DAPHNE DU MAURIER (1907–1989)

Always read stuff that will make you look good if you die in the middle of the night.

ATTRIBUTED TO P. J. O'ROURKE (1947–   )

There is no reason why the same man should like the same books at eighteen and at forty-eight.

EZRA POUND
ABC OF READING (1934)

If I weren't out there every day battling the white man, I could spend the rest of my life reading.

MALCOLM X (1925–1965)

One is brought into a milieu that does not exist, but which, over the course of reading, one gets accustomed to and which, in one way or the other, one recognizes. It becomes real, intrusive and capturing and finally, uncompromising and intimate: like a mirror.

HARRY MARTINSON (1904–1978)

I have sometimes dreamt . . . that when the Day of Judgement dawns and the great conquerors and lawyers and statesmen come to receive their rewards . . . the Almighty will . . . say, not without a certain envy when He sees us coming with our books under our arms, "Look, these need no reward. We have nothing to give them here. They have loved reading."

VIRGINIA WOOLF
THE COMMON READER (1932)

People say that life is the thing, but I prefer reading.

LOGAN PEARSALL SMITH
AFTERTHOUGHTS (1931)

Only in books has mankind known perfect truth, love and beauty.

GEORGE BERNARD SHAW (1856–1950)

No reading should be compulsory.

JULIAN BARNES (1946–   )

The world may be full of fourth-rate writers, but it's also full of fourth-rate readers.

STAN BARSTOW (1928–   )

Men do not understand BOOKS until they have had a certain amount of life.

EZRA POUND
ABC OF READING (1934)

It is curious how tyrannical the habit of reading is, and what shifts we make to escape thinking. There is no bore we dread being left with so much as our own minds.

ROBERT LOWELL (1917–1977)

To search the book, and in the warming air

Parted its dripping leaves with eager care.

Strange matters did it treat of, and drew on

My soul page after page, till well-nigh won

Into forgetfulness; when, stupefied,

I read these words, and read again, and tried

My eyes against the heavens, and read again.

JOHN KEATS
ENDYMION: A POETIC ROMANCE (1818)

———

My own words, when I am at work on a story, I hear too as they go, in the same voice that I hear when I read in books. When I write and the sound of it comes back to my ears, then I act to make changes. I have always trusted this voice.

EUDORA WELTY
ONE WRITER'S BEGINNINGS (1984)

Whatever value there is in studying literature, cultural or practical, comes from the total body of our reading, the castle of words we've built, and keep adding new wings to it all the time. As for us, we can't even speak or think or comprehend even our own experience except within the limits of our own power over words, and those limits have been established for us by our great writers.

NORTHROP FRYE
THE EDUCATED IMAGINATION (1964)

Wordstruck is exactly what I was—and still am: crazy about the sound of words, the look of words, the taste of words, the feeling for words on the tongue and in the mind.

ROBERT MACNEIL
WORDSTRUCK (1989)

Of all the needs a book has, the chief need is that it be readable.

>ANTHONY TROLLOPE (1815–1882)
>
>*AN AUTOBIOGRAPHY* (1883)

In reading, one should notice and fondle details.

>VLADIMIR NABOKOV (1899–1977)
>
>IN FREDSON BOWERS, ED., *LECTURES ON LITERATURE* (1980-1981)

One feels like crawling on all fours after reading your work.

>VOLTAIRE
>
>IN A LETTER TO ROUSSEAU (AUGUST 3, 1761)

Digressions, incontestably, are the sunshine—they are the life, the soul of reading.

>LAURENCE STERNE
>
>*TRISTRAM SHANDY* (1759–1767)

You write with ease to show your breeding,
But easy writing's curst hard reading.

> RICHARD SHERIDAN
> *CLIO'S PROTEST* (1819)

My argument is that War makes rattling good history, but Peace is poor reading.

> THOMAS HARDY
> "SPIRIT SINISTER"
> *THE DYNASTS* (1903–1908)

There is no accident in our choice of reading. All our sources are related.

> FRANÇOIS MAURIAC
> *MÉMOIRES INTÉRIEURES* (1959)

You may perhaps be brought to acknowledge that it is very well worthwhile to be tormented for two or three years of one's life, for the sake of being able to read all the rest of it.

JANE AUSTEN
NORTHANGER ABBEY (1818)

I've never known any troubles that an hour's reading didn't assuage.

CHARLES DE MONTESQUIEU (1689–1755)

Reading has a history.

ROBERT DARNTON (1939–   )

Read in order to Live.

GUSTAVE FLAUBERT
IN A LETTER TO MADEMOISELLE DE CHANTEPIC (JUNE 1857)

For the desire to read, like all the other desires that distract our unhappy souls, is capable of analysis.

> VIRGINA WOOLF
> "SIR THOMAS BROWNE" (1923)

Reading means approaching something that is just coming into being.

> ITALO CALVINO
> *IF ON A WINTER'S NIGHT A TRAVELLER* (1981)

One must be an inventor to read well.

> RALPH WALDO EMERSON
> "THE AMERICAN SCHOLAR" (1837)

5

Libraries

Libraries are an essential part of the culture of books. Anyone willing to fill out the form for a library card is afforded the wisdom and pleasure they have to offer. Public libraries are among the few remaining institutions that provide an important, free service for everyone, regardless of financial status.

Bring your questions to any good library, and most likely you will match them up with answers. Bring loneliness, and in books you will find the solace and company of other lives. Bring the gray of the everyday and you will lose it in the infinite colors of books. The great houses and protectors of books, libraries offer as many thousands of worlds as there are volumes on their shelves; these quotes are a testament to one of our most important public institutions.

H.H.

What is more important in a library than anything else—than everything else—is the fact that it exists.

ARCHIBALD MACLEISH
"THE PREMISE OF MEANING"
AMERICAN SCHOLAR (JUNE 5, 1972)

To an historian libraries are food, shelter and even muse. They are of two kinds: the library of published material, books, pamphlets, periodicals, and the archive of unpublished papers and documents.

BARBARA TUCHMAN
PRACTICING HISTORY (1981)

Libraries are reservoirs of strength, grace and wit, reminders of order, calm and continuity, lakes of mental energy, neither warm nor cold, light nor dark. The pleasure they give is steady, unorgastic, reliable, deep and long-lasting. In any library in the world, I am at home, unselfconscious, still and absorbed.

GERMAINE GREER
DADDY, WE HARDLY KNEW YOU (1989)

I've always found them close relatives of the walking dead.

ALAN BENNETT
IN ANTHONY THWAITE, *LARKIN AT SIXTY* (1982)

———

As library annual reports have indicated for some time—here one need only cite, for example, the famous passage found in column 1,303 of the Annual Report of the Library at Alexandria for 250 B.C.—the disappearance, exchange, and loss of umbrellas is a phenomenon closely associated with libraries.

NORMAN D. STEVENS
"THE UMBRELLA PAPER" (1980)

———

Tough choices face the biblioholic at every step of the way—like choosing between reading and eating, between buying new clothes and buying books, between a reasonable lifestyle and one of penurious but masochistic happiness lived out in the wallow of excess.

TOM RAABE
BIBLIOHOLISM: THE LITERARY ADDICTION (1991)

Medicine for the soul.

INSCRIPTION OVER THE DOOR OF THE LIBRARY AT THEBES

"Captain Nemo," said I to my host, who had just thrown himself on one of the divans, "this is a library which would do honor to more than one of the continental palaces, and I am absolutely astounded when I consider that it can follow you to the bottom of the sea."

"Where could one find greater solitude or silence, Professor?" replied Captain Nemo. "Did your study in the Museum afford you such perfect quiet?"

JULES VERNE
20,000 LEAGUES UNDER THE SEA (1870)

I'll never understand it—all these books—a world of knowledge at your fingertips—and you play poker all night.

MORGAN FREEMAN
AS DETECTIVE SOMERSET IN THE MOVIE SEVEN (1995)

Just because the f—er's got a library card doesn't make him Yoda.

BRAD PITT
AS DETECTIVE MILLS IN THE MOVIE *SEVEN* (1995)

"If none but true and useful things were recorded, our immense historical libraries would be reduced to a very narrow compass; but we should know more and know it better.

VOLTAIRE (1694–1778)

For I bless God in the libraries of the learned and for all the booksellers in the world.

CHRISTOPHER SMART (1722–1771)

Books are a world in themselves, it is true; but they are not the only world. The world is a volume larger than all the libraries in it.

THOMAS HARDY (1840–1928)

Perhaps no place in any community is so totally democratic as the town library. The only entrance requirement is interest.

LADY BIRD JOHNSON (1912–   )

How delightful to stop reading and look out! How stimulating the scene is, in its unconsciousness, its irrelevance, its perpetual movement—the colts galloping round the field, the woman filling her pail at the well, the donkey throwing back his head and emitting his long, acrid moan. The greater part of any library is nothing but the record of such fleeting moments in the lives of men, women, and donkeys.

VIRGINIA WOOLF
THE COMMON READER (1932)

If this nation is to be wise as well as strong, if we are to achieve our destiny, then we need more new ideas for more wise men reading more good books in more public libraries.

JOHN F. KENNEDY (1917–1963)

The true university of these days is a collection of books.

THOMAS CARLYLE
ON HEROES AND HERO-WORSHIP (1841)

Instead of going to Paris to attend lectures, go to the public library, and you won't come out for twenty years, if you really wish to learn.

LEO TOLSTOY (1828–1910)

Libraries keep the records on behalf of all humanity . . . the unique and the absurd, the wise and fragment of stupidity.

VARTAN GREGORIAN (1935–)

What in the world would we do without our libraries?

KATHARINE HEPBURN (1909–)

He that revels in a well-chosen library, has innumerable dishes and all of admirable flavor.

WILLIAM GODWIN (1756–1836)

I've been drunk for about a week now, and I thought it might sober me up to sit in a library.

F. SCOTT FITZGERALD
THE GREAT GATSBY (1925)

I ransack public libraries, and find them full of sunk treasure.

VIRGINIA WOOLF (1882–1941)
IN HERMIONE LEE, *VIRGINIA WOOLF* (1996)

No place affords a more striking conviction of the vanity of human hopes than a public library.

SAMUEL JOHNSON
IN *THE RAMBLER* (MARCH 23, 1751)

What do we, as a nation, care about books? How much do you think we spend altogether on our libraries, public or private, as compared with what we spend on our horses?

JOHN RUSKIN
SESAME AND LILIES (1865)

My library
was dukedom large enough.

WILLIAM SHAKESPEARE
THE TEMPEST (1611–1612)

6

Literacy

The term "literacy" refers to many modes of understanding: cultural literacy, computer literacy, functional literacy, numerical literacy, to name a few—or simply basic reading and writing skills that offer us the ability to access, and communicate through, written language. As such, literacy remains a fundamental building block of citizenship.

A few years ago, I taught basic reading and writing skills to a group of adults who were all coping with serious and persistent mental illnesses. Most of them, at the peak of their learning capacity as youths, had been ostracized from their society, hidden away in state hospitals for decades, deprived of what would have allowed them to become functional, active citizens. Not only had they been removed from their families and locked away in wards, denied the chance to fight their mental illness, but they also had been denied a basic means of communication.

As they learned to read and write, these people underwent changes that were wonderful to see. They learned to deal with their initial shame about not knowing what they believed every other adult knew. They grew passionate about mastering the use of language. And they proved, powerfully, our basic need to communicate through written symbols—a tool we use throughout our lives, and that can often initiate dramatic change.

H.H.

She began the first of what we later called "my lessons in living." She said that I must always be intolerant of ignorance but understanding of illiteracy.

MAYA ANGELOU
I KNOW WHY THE CAGED BIRD SINGS (1970)

———•··•———

The man who does not read good books has no advantage over the man who can't read them.

MARK TWAIN (1835–1910)

———•··•———

You must get into the habit of looking intensely at words, and assuring yourself of their meaning . . . you might read all the books in the British Museum (if you could live long enough) and remain an utterly "illiterate," un-educated person; but if you read ten pages of a good book . . . you are for ever more in some measure an educated person.

JOHN RUSKIN (1819–1900)

Rousseau points out the facility with which children lend themselves to our false methods . . . "The apparent ease with which children learn is their ruin."

E. D. HIRSCH
CULTURAL LITERACY (1987)

Cultural literacy constitutes the only sure avenue of opportunity for disadvantaged children, the only reliable way of combating the social determinants that now condemn them to remain in the same social and educational condition as their parents.

E. D. HIRSCH
CULTURAL LITERACY (1987)

To be truly literate, citizens must be able to grasp the meaning of any piece of writing addressed to the general reader.

E. D. HIRSCH
CULTURAL LITERACY (1987)

Were it left to me to decide whether we should have a government without newspapers, or newspapers without a government, I should not hesitate a moment to prefer the latter. But I should mean that every man should receive those papers and be capable of reading them.

THOMAS JEFFERSON (1743–1826)

The difference between the literate person as an Object and as Subject is social and political, not individual. It requires a look at who else is involved and how, and at the role and power of the literate in relation to the role and power of the other(s). Ultimately, it refers to the amount of control a person has over the print-use and the conduct of the literacy event.

CAROLE EDELSKY

For newly freed slaves, going to school, learning to read and write, were essential steps in the process of freedom.

JAMES W. FRASER (1944–   )

Freedom is not merely the chance to do as one pleases; neither is it merely the opportunity to choose between set alternatives. Freedom is, first of all, the chance to formulate the available choices, to argue over them—and then the opportunity to choose. That is why freedom cannot exist without an enlarged role of human reason in human affairs.

C. WRIGHT MILLS (1916–1962)

Literacy salvaged my life. It is as simple and fundamental as that.

SHARON JEAN HAMILTON

The state of literacy in the United States today is declining so precipitously, while video and computer technologies are becoming so powerful that the act of reading itself may well be on the way to obsolescence.

JANET E. HEALY

The kinds of make-believe writing and reading children bring into their play can tell us a great deal about how and when literacy begins.

JEROME BRUNER
ACTS OF MEANING (1970)

Central to many recent discussions of literacy is the notion that writing and reading are ways of making, interpreting, and communicating meaning.

JEROME BRUNER
ACTS OF MEANING (1970)

The notion of multiple literacies recognized that there are many ways of being—and of becoming—literate, and that how literacy develops and how it is used depend on the particular social and cultural setting.

JEROME BRUNER
ACTS OF MEANING (1970)

Literacy is a social and cultural achievement, as well as a cognitive one.

JEROME BRUNER
ACTS OF MEANING (1970)

I'm quite illiterate, but I read a lot.

J. D. SALINGER (1919–   )

Even if, before this century, all or most or a majority of the children had the benefit of primary or elementary schooling, that could not be expected to achieve more than a rudimentary literacy and numeracy.

MORTIMER J. ADLER (1902–   )

What is it to be literate? . . . Our literacy, autobiographies reveal riches and gaps, but these narratives are not tales of solitary journeys. We were always in dialogue with others—those who taught us to read, those for whom we wrote, who lent us books, shaped our preferences, encouraged us, forbade us even. They were dead poets, living authors, cynical critics. We remember them as friends who made our world more habitable, who helped us, as we read and wrote, to discover who we were and who we could become.

MARGARET MEEK

7

Censorship and the Destruction of Books

As long as there have been books, there have been those who proclaimed that certain ones were either unfit or unsuitable to be read, even dangerous. The implication, of course, is that some censor in authority knows best. From the quotations on this topic, it is clear that censorship and the destruction of books is of immense importance to both writers and readers. John Milton found censorship so threatening that he could write, in his great defense of a free press, "Areopagitica," "as good almost kill a man as kill a good book; who kills a man kills a reasonable creature, God's image, but he who destroys a good book, kills reason itself."

From the Enlightenment and Pierre de Beaumarchais to the Soviet Gulag of Solzhenitsyn, writers have feared and fought those forces that would attempt to prevent the printed exchange of ideas.

Deep down inside, everyone wants to ban something.

> ALAN M. DERSHOWITZ (1938–   )

Congress shall make no law . . . abridging the freedom of speech, or of the press.

> AMENDMENT I
> U.S. CONSTITUTION

Wherever they burn books they will also, in the end, burn human beings.

> HEINRICH HEINE
> *ALMANSOR* (1823)

Books cannot be killed by fire. People die, but books never die. No man and no force can abolish memory . . . In this war, we know, books are weapons.

> FRANKLIN DELANO ROOSEVELT
> MESSAGE TO THE AMERICAN BOOKSELLERS ASSOCIATION
>   (APRIL 23, 1942)

Even bad books are books, and therefore sacred.

GÜNTHER GRASS
THE TIN DRUM (1959)

Assassination is the extreme form of censorship.

GEORGE BERNARD SHAW
THE REJECTED STATEMENT

A great writer is, so to speak, a second government in his country. And for that reason no regime has ever loved great writers, only minor ones.

ALEXANDER SOLZHENITSYN
THE FIRST CIRCLE (1968)

If there is a bedrock principle underlying the First Amendment, it is that the government may not prohibit the expression of an idea simply because society finds the idea itself offensive or disagreeable.

U.S. SUPREME COURT JUSTICE WILLIAM J. BRENNAN JR. (1906–1997)

Don't join the book burners. Don't think you are going to conceal faults by concealing evidence that they ever existed. Don't be afraid to go in your library and read every book.

DWIGHT D. EISENHOWER (1890–1969)

In the long run of history, the censor and the inquisitor have always lost. The only sure weapon against bad ideas is better ideas.

ALFRED WHITNEY GRISWOLD (1906–1963)

It is not my experience that society hates and fears the writer, or that society adulates the writer. Instead my experience is the common one, that society places the writer so far beyond the pale that society does not regard the writer at all.

ANNIE DILLARD (1945–   )

I think we ought to read only the kind of books that wound and stab us.

FRANZ KAFKA (1883–1924)
IN A LETTER TO OSKAR POLLACK

If you're ready, as a lawyer, to defend even murderers, why don't you come to the defense of writers who have committed no wrong except for writing books?

MILAN KUNDERA
IMMORTALITY (1991)

. . . unless wariness be used, as good almost kill a man as kill a good book; who kills a man kills a reasonable creature, God's image, but he who destroys a good book, kills reason itself.

JOHN MILTON
"AREOPAGITICA" (1644)

And more from John Milton, in "Areopagitica," on the logic and necessity for a free press:

> To the pure all things are pure, not only meats and drinks, but all kind of knowledge whether good or evil; the knowledge cannot defile, nor consequently the books, if the will and conscience be not defiled.

And still more:

> I cannot praise a fugitive and cloistered virtue, unexercised and unbreathed, that never sallies out and sees her adversary but slinks out of the race, where that immortal garland is to be run for, not without dust and heat.

Truth is not taught by laws, nor has she any need of force to procure her entrance into the minds of men. Errors indeed prevail by the assistance of foreign and borrowed succors. But if truth makes not her way into the understanding by her own light, she will be the weaker for any borrowed force violence can add to her.

JOHN LOCKE (1632–1704)

I reject the insolence of self-righteous moralistic fund-raising politicians or politically ambitious priests in using my poetry as a political football for their quasi-religious agendas. I have my own agenda for emotional and intellectual and political liberty in the U.S.A. and behind the Iron Curtain. This is expressed in my poetry.

ALLEN GINSBERG (1926–1997)

Our civilization cannot afford to let the censor-moron loose. The censor-moron does not really hate anything but the living and growing human consciousness. It is our developing and extending consciousness that he threatens—and our consciousness is its newest, most sensitive activity, its vital growth. To arrest or circumscribe the vital consciousness is to produce morons, and nothing but a moron would do it.

D. H. LAWRENCE (1885–1930)

There are worse crimes than burning books. One of them is not reading them.

JOSEPH BRODSKY (1940–1996)

The reaction to any word may be, in any individual, either a mob-reaction or an individual reaction. It is up to the individual to ask himself: Is my reaction individual, or am I merely reacting from my mob-self? When it comes to the so-called obscene words, I should say that hardly one person in a million escapes mob-reaction.

D. H. LAWRENCE (1885–1930)

Today the full conscious realization of sex is even more important than the act itself. After centuries of obfuscation, the mind demands to know and know fully.

D. H. LAWRENCE (1885–1930)

There are many who lust for the simple answers of doctrine or degree. They are on the left and right. They are not confined to a single part of society. They are terrorists of the mind.

A. BARTLETT GIAMATTI (1938–1989)

Express everything you like. No word can hurt you. None. No idea can hurt you. Not being able to express an idea or a word will hurt you much more. As much as a bullet.

JAMAICA KINCAID (1949–   )

I can't get upset about "offensive to women" or "offensive to blacks" or "offensive to Native Americans" or "offensive to Jews" . . . Offend! I can't get worked up about it. Offend!

JAMAICA KINCAID (1949–   )

God forbid that any book should be banned. The practice is as indefensible as infanticide.

REBECCA WEST
THE STRANGE NECESSITY (1928)

The author of the *Satanic Verses* book, which is against Islam, the Prophet, and the Koran, and all those involved in its publication who were aware of its content, are sentenced to death. I ask all Moslems to execute them wherever they find them.

RUHOLLA KHOMEINI
FATWA AGAINST SALMAN RUSHDIE (FEBRUARY 14, 1989)

I call upon the intellectual community in this country and abroad to stand up for freedom of the imagination, an issue much larger than my book or indeed my life.

SALMAN RUSHDIE (1947–   )

I don't think pornography is very harmful, but it is terribly, terribly boring.

NOEL COWARD (1899–1973)

The condition every art requires is, not so much freedom from restriction, as freedom from adulteration and from the intrusion of foreign matter.

WILLA CATHER (1873–1947)

Every burned book or house enlightens the world; every suppressed or expunged word reverberates through the earth from side to side.

RALPH WALDO EMERSON (1803–1882)

We do not fear censorship for we have no wish to offend with improprieties or obscenities, but we do demand, as a right, the liberty to show the dark side of wrong, that we may illuminate the bright side of virtue—the same liberty that is conceded to the art of the written word, that art to which we owe the Bible and the works of Shakespeare.

D. W. GRIFFITH (1875–1948)

The crime of book purging is that it involves a rejection of the word. For the word is never absolute truth, but only man's frail and human effort to approach the truth. To reject the word is to reject the human search.

MAX LERNER
IN *THE NEW YORK POST* (JUNE 24, 1953)

We live in oppressive times. We have, as a nation, become our own thought police; but instead of calling the process by which we limit our expression of dissent and wonder "censorship," we call it "concern for viability."

DAVID MAMET (1947–   )

If some books are deemed most baneful and their sale forbid, how, then, with deadlier facts, not dreams of doting men? Those whom books will hurt will not be proof against events. Events, not books, should be forbid.

HERMAN MELVILLE (1819–1891)

Instead of asking—"How much damage will the work in question bring about?" why not ask—"How much good? How much joy?"

HENRY MILLER
THE AIR-CONDITIONED NIGHTMARE (1945)

Art is never chaste. It ought to be forbidden to ignorant innocents, never allowed into contact with those not sufficiently prepared. Yes, art is dangerous. Where it is chaste, it is not art.

PABLO PICASSO (1881–1973)

And art made tongue-tied by authority.

WILLIAM SHAKESPEARE (1564–1616)
SONNET 66

Woe to that nation whose literature is cut short by the intrusion of force. This is not merely interference with freedom of the press but the sealing up of a nation's heart, the excision of its memory.

ALEXANDER SOLZHENITSYN
IN *TIME* (FEBRUARY 25, 1974)

All fiction . . . is censored in the interest of the ruling class.

GEORGE ORWELL
IN *HORIZON* (MARCH 1940)

I think you can leave the arts, superior or inferior, to the conscience of mankind.

W. B. YEATS
SPEECH IN THE IRISH SENATE (1923)

The violence and obscenity are left unadulterated, as manifestation of the mystery and pain which ever accompanies the act of creation.

ANAÏS NIN (1903–1977)

If censorship reigns there cannot be sincere flattery, and only small men are afraid of small writings.

PIERRE DE BEAUMARCHAIS
THE MARRIAGE OF FIGARO (1784)

I suppose that writers should, in a way, feel flattered by the censorship laws. They show a primitive fear and dread at the fearful magic of print.

JOHN MORTIMER
CLINGING TO THE WRECKAGE (1982)

The free expression of the hopes and aspirations of a people is the greatest and only safety in a sane society.

EMMA GOLDMAN (1869–1940)

To admit authorities, however heavily furred and gowned, into our libraries and let them tell us how to read, what to read, what value to place upon what we read, is to destroy the spirit of freedom which is the breath of those sanctuaries. Everywhere else we may be bound by laws and conventions—there we have none.

VIRGINIA WOOLF
THE COMMON READER (1932)

Censorship may have to do with literature, but literature has nothing whatever to do with censorship.

> NADINE GORDIMER (1923–)

I disapprove of what you say, but will defend to the death your right to say it.

> S. G. TALLENTYRE

Books being once called in and forbidden become more salable and public.

> MICHEL DE MONTAIGNE
> *ESSAYS*, Vol. III (1580)

Well! it is now public, and you will stand for your privileges we know: to read, and censure. Do so, but buy it first. That doth best commend a book, the stationer says.

> WILLIAM SHAKESPEARE (1564–1616)
> PREFACE TO THE FIRST FOLIO

Much malice mingled with a little wit. Perhaps may censure this mysterious writ.

> JOHN DRYDEN
> *THE HIND AND THE PANTHER* (1687)

So total is the present system of bureaucratic control of culture, so perfect the surveillance of every chink through which some major work might see the light of day, so greatly does that little band of men, who hold the keys to every door in their own pockets, fear the government and fear art.

> VÁCLAV HAVEL (1936–   )

The one thing they did not—and could not—stop me doing was to write the officially permitted, naturally censored, letters to my wife.

> VÁCLAV HAVEL (1936–   )

Literature is the one place in any society where, within the secrecy of our own heads, we can hear voices talking about everything in every possible way. The reason for ensuring that privileged arena is preserved is not that writers want the absolute freedom to say and do whatever they please. It is that we, all of us, readers and writers and citizens and generals and godmen, need that little, unimportant-looking room. We do not need to call it sacred, but we need to remember that it is necessary.

SALMAN RUSHDIE
"IS NOTHING SACRED" (1990)

Everybody knows there is no fineness or accuracy of suppression. If you hold down one thing, you hold down the adjoining.

SAUL BELLOW
THE ADVENTURES OF AUGIE MARCH (1953)

On turning books into movies—a kind of book burning. [Mr. DeMille said] "Ah yes, zebras in the *King of Kings*." So I went back to my office and I got a Bible and I felt what in heaven's name are zebras doing in that picture about the life of Christ. I thought, maybe he said "Hebrews"?

DOROTHY PARKER
"HOLLYWOOD, THE LAND I WON'T RETURN TO" (1955)

Wherever in the world the little room of literature has been closed, sooner or later the walls have come tumbling down.

SALMAN RUSHDIE (1947–   )

If all mankind minus one were of one opinion, and only one person were of the contrary opinion, mankind would be no more justified in silencing that one person, than he, if he has the power, would be justified in silencing mankind.

JOHN STUART MILL
ON LIBERTY (1859)

The peculiar evil of silencing the expression of an opinion is, that it is robbing the human race; posterity as well as the existing generation; those who dissent from the opinion, still more than those who hold it. If the opinion is right, they are deprived of the opportunity of exchanging error for truth: if wrong, they lose, what is almost as great a benefit, the clearer perception and livelier impression of truth, produced by its collision with error.

JOHN STUART MILL
ON LIBERTY (1859)

A book cannot be proscribed unless it is found to be utterly without redeeming social value.

U.S. SUPREME COURT JUSTICE WILLIAM J. BRENNAN JR. (1906–1997)

Anyone who acts as if freedom's defenses are to be found in suppression and suspicion and fear confesses a doctrine that is alien to America.

DWIGHT D. EISENHOWER (1890–1969)

Certain strong and eager minds embrace original opinions, seldom all wrong, never quite true, but of a mixed sort, part truth, part error . . . The truth has the best of the proof, and therefore wins most of the judgments. The process is slow . . . Time in it is reckoned not by days, but by years . . . Yet on the whole it creeps along, if you do not stop it. But all is arrested if persecution begins.

WALTER BAGEHOT (1826–1877)

8

Publishing and Publishers

There has long been a love-hate relationship between authors and their publishers. While each agrees that one could not exist without the other, it frequently is not a relationship of mutual admiration and respect, to say the least. Few writers acknowledge their great debts to those who have published their work, and even fewer publishers acknowledge how dependent their lists are upon the writers whom they have published.

The quotations that follow include words from some of the greatest editors of American letters (Maxwell Perkins) and British literature (Colin Haycroft), along with those of Harold Ross (a magazine editor) and such great writers as V. S. Pritchett, Cyril Connolly, Ernest Hemingway, and Raymond Chandler. Often the author projects shattered hopes of critical acclaim and monetary riches, and the publisher regrets never having gotten credit for the commercial success he feels he deserves. We are left with a trove of comments that offer tremendous insight into the industry of books, one that has often been called—ironically— the "gentleman's profession."

No man is a genius to his publisher.

HEINRICH HEINE (1797–1856)

It is easy to become a publisher, but difficult to remain one; the mortality in infancy is higher than in any other trade or profession.

SIR STANLEY UNWIN
THE TRUTH ABOUT PUBLISHING (1960)

The minute you try to talk business with him he takes the attitude that he is a gentleman and a scholar, and the moment you try to approach him on the level of his moral integrity he starts to talk business.

RAYMOND CHANDLER
RAYMOND CHANDLER SPEAKING (1962)

I read and re-read this article again and again and then, as happens to writers, I was impatient with it and disliked it. I had my first experience of the depression and sense of nothingness that comes when a piece of work is done. The satisfaction is in the act itself.

V. S. PRITCHETT
MIDNIGHT OIL (1971)

To John, I ow'd great obligation;
But John, unhappily, thought fit
To publish it to all the nation:
Sure John and I are more than quit.

MATTHEW PRIOR
"EPIGRAM" (1718)

A publisher is a specialized form of bank or building society, catering for customers who cannot cope with life and are therefore forced to write about it.

COLIN HAYCROFT (1929–1994)

Publish and be damned.

ATTRIBUTED TO ARTHUR WELLESLEY, DUKE OF WELLINGTON
(1769–1852)
(REPLY TO A BLACKMAIL THREAT)

A best-seller is the golden touch of mediocre talent.

CYRIL CONNOLLY (1903–1974)

The principle of procrastinated rape is said to be the ruling one in all the great best-sellers.

V. S. PRITCHETT
THE LIVING NOVEL (1947)

Hype springs eternal in every publisher's breast.

COLIN HAYCROFT (1929–1994)

Having books published is very destructive to writing. It is even worse than making love too much. Because when you make love too much at least you get a damned clarity that is like no other light. A very clear and hollow light.

ERNEST HEMINGWAY (1899–1961)

The portability of the book, like that of the easel painting, added much to the new cult of individualism.

MARSHALL MCLUHAN
THE GUTENBERG GALAXY (1962)

When you publish a book it's the world's book. The world edits it.

PHILIP ROTH (1933–)
IN *NEW YORK TIMES BOOK REVIEW* (SEPTEMBER 2, 1979)

Publishers are notoriously slothful about numbers, unless they're attached to dollar signs—unlike journalists, quarterbacks, and felony criminal defendants who tend to be keenly aware of numbers at all times.

HUNTER S. THOMPSON
SONGS OF THE DOOMED (1990)

Editing is the same thing as quarrelling with writers—same thing exactly.

HAROLD ROSS
IN *TIME* (MARCH 6, 1950)

Books are the curse of the human race. Nine-tenths of existing books are nonsense, and the clever books are the refutation of that nonsense. The greatest misfortune that ever befell man was the invention of printing.

BENJAMIN DISRAELI (1804–1881)

I suppose publishers are untrustworthy. They certainly always look it.

OSCAR WILDE (1854–1900)

Publishers are not necessarily either philanthropists or rogues. Likewise, they are usually neither lordly magnates nor cringing beggars. As a working hypothesis, regard them as ordinary human beings trying to earn their living at an unusually difficult occupation.

SIR STANLEY UNWIN
THE TRUTH ABOUT PUBLISHING (1960)

Only one thing is impossible for God: to find any sense in any copyright law in the planet.

MARK TWAIN
NOTEBOOK (MAY 23, 1910)

An editor does not add to a book. At best he serves as a handmaiden to an author. Don't ever get to feeling important about yourself, because an editor at most releases energy. He creates nothing.

MAXWELL PERKINS (1884–1947)

University printing presses exist, and are subsidised by the Government for the purpose of producing books which no one can read; and they are true to their high calling.

F. M. CORNFORD
MICROCOSMOGRAPHIA ACADEMICA (1908)

All a publisher has to do is write checques at intervals, while a lot of deserving and industrious chappies rally round and do the real work.

P. G. WODEHOUSE (1881–1975)

Publishers and printers alike seemed to agree among themselves, no matter how divergent their points of view were in other matters, not to publish anything of mine as I wrote it.

JAMES JOYCE
LETTER (APRIL 2, 1932)

As repressed sadists are supposed to become policemen or butchers, so those with an irrational fear of life become publishers.

CYRIL CONNOLLY
ENEMIES OF PROMISE (1938)

You cannot or at least you should not try to argue with authors. Too many are like children whose tears can suddenly be changed to smiles if they are handled in the right way.

MICHAEL JOSEPH
THE ADVENTURE OF PUBLISHING (1949)

American publishers and editors have done their utmost to destroy taste, passion, and discrimination in the reading public.

HENRY MILLER
"WHEN I REACH FOR MY REVOLVER" (1955)

Publishing is merely a matter of saying Yes and No at the right time.

MICHAEL JOSEPH
SPEECH AT FOYLE'S JUBILEE DINNER (1954)

The lions looked like so many publishers satiated on a diet of mutual agreement over terms.

PAUL SCOTT
LETTER (JUNE 15, 1968)

Publishers are in business to make money, and if your books do well they don't care if you are male, female, or an elephant.

> MARGARET ATWOOD
> IN "DISSECTING THE WAY A WRITER WORKS"
> *ELEVEN CANADIAN NOVELISTS* (1973)

If your publisher promises you a full-page ad in the *New York Times*, get it in writing.

> BILL ADLER
> *INSIDE PUBLISHING* (1982)

A publisher who writes is like a cow in a milk bar.

> ATTRIBUTED TO ARTHUR KOESTLER (1905–1983)

The chief qualification of ninety-nine per cent of all editors is failure. They have failed as writers . . . If I fail as a writer, I shall have proved for the career of editorship. There's bread and butter and jam, at any rate.

JACK LONDON
MARTIN EDEN (1909)

I suppose some editors are failed writers—but so are most writers.

T. S. ELIOT (1888–1965)

It is not wise to solicit the opinions of publishers—they become proud if you do.

GORE VIDAL
IN GEORGE GREENFIELD, *SCRIBBLERS FOR BREAD* (1989)

Four happy publishers
Out on a spree.
Someone had to pay the bill
Then there were three

WENDY COPE
"TWO-HAND RHYMES FOR GROWN-UPS" (1992)

It's an editor's world. However cross an editor makes you, you cannot afford to quarrel. Swear after you've put the phone down and not before.

SUSAN ELKIN
IN BARRY TURNER, *THE WRITER'S COMPANION* (1996)

I'm not saying all publishers have to be literary, but *some* interest in books would help.

A. N. WILSON
IN *BOOKSELLER* (JULY 5, 1996)

A person who publishes a book appears willfully in public with his pants down.

EDNA ST. VINCENT MILLAY (1892–1950)

Publication is the auction
Of the mind of man.

EMILY DICKINSON (1830–1886)

Though our publishers will tell you that they are ever seeking "original" writers, nothing could be farther from the truth. What they want is more of the same, only thinly disguised. They most certainly do not want another Faulkner, another Melville, another Thoreau, another Whitman. What the *public* wants, no one knows. Not even the publishers.

HENRY MILLER
"WHEN I REACH FOR MY REVOLVER" (1955)

I frankly worry less about those who have already published and become known than I do about those who haven't yet published anything and who still can't today, not because their names are blacklisted—they couldn't possibly be, for the simple reason that they haven't made a name for themselves yet—but because what they write does not fit into the narrow framework of what, today, is possible and publishable.

VÁCLAV HAVEL (1936–   )

A copy of verses kept in the cabinet, and only shown to a few friends, is like a virgin much sought after and admired; but when printed and published, is like a common whore, whom anybody may purchase for half-a-crown.

JONATHAN SWIFT (1667–1745)

Books, after all, are extraordinary things: thoughts made visible, paper and ink sculptures of the mind, time and space made into words. There's no end to judging so many books. But a literary editor's work is never what Ecclesiastes calls a weariness of the flesh. Rather, it's an animation of the spirit.

DANIEL JOHNSON

The printing-press is either the greatest blessing or the greatest curse of modern times, one sometimes forgets which.

J. M. BARRIE (1860–1937)

Night and Day will be out shortly, Gerald Duckworth lost the last chapter, so I daresay it will be November instead of October. I don't feel nervous; nobody cares a hang what one writes, and novels are such clumsy and half extinct monsters at the best.

VIRGINIA WOOLF (1882–1941)

I'm trying to finish off, and send to the printer . . . I should very much like to be edited by you . . . you will not only have to fix the length—you will have to be sincere, and severe . . . I shall respect you all the more for tearing me up and throwing me into the wastepaper basket.

VIRGINIA WOOLF (1882–1941)

It's no joke publishing one's own book.

VIRGINIA WOOLF (1882–1941)

English publishers being what they are (i.e., chary about wasting stamps), I never get to find out what the press says about any book of mine until years later, and then only in red ink on the publisher's statement.

S. J. PERELMAN
LETTER (JULY 7, 1960)

The most important difference between poetry and any other department of publishing is, that whereas with most categories of books you are aiming to make as much money as possible, with poetry you are aiming to lose as little as possible.

T. S. ELIOT (1888–1965)

It's the old Catch-22; you can never get an agent unless you're published, and when you most need one, you can't have one.

C. J. CHERRYH
QUOTED IN *WORDSMITHS OF WONDER*

Every morning a snowy avalanche of manuscripts swelled the dust-gray piles in the office of the Fiction Editor. Secretly, in studies and attics and schoolrooms all over America, people must be writing. Say someone or other finished a manuscript every minute; in five minutes that would be five manuscripts stacked on the Fiction Editor's desk. Within the hour there would be sixty, crowding each other onto the floor.

SYLVIA PLATH
THE BELL JAR (1963)

Nothing stinks like a pile of unpublished writing.

SYLVIA PLATH
THE BELL JAR (1963)

The unpublished manuscript is like an unconfessed sin that festers in the soul, corrupting and contaminating it.

ANTONIO MACHADO (1875–1939)

For several days after my first book was published, I carried it about in my pocket, and took surreptitious looks at it to make sure that the ink had not faded.

J. M. BARRIE
SPEECH AT CRITIC'S CIRCLE IN LONDON (MAY 26, 1922)

Still, the E-book is not a passing thing, but here to stay as it becomes cheaper and improved. Nonetheless, it is really no more than a screen upon which to read, and it is clear that when enough people start reading them, electronic books will do for the ophthalmologists what taffy and caramels did for dentists.

MARTIN ARNOLD
IN *THE NEW YORK TIMES* (JANUARY 7, 1999)

Over 1 Million Additional Titles Available to Ship in 24 Hours. Includes 50,000 Publishers.

SIGN IN BARNES & NOBLE WINDOW (1999)

9

Literature

"Literature" and "classic" can be fearful words, carrying with them the implication of musty tomes that offer more to the reader in their reputation than in actual enjoyment. But if Ezra Pound is correct when he says that "Literature is news that STAYS news," such writing should remain fresh for succeeding generations, always capable of giving readers pleasure and wisdom. And so it does.

Throughout this section, you will find that underlying theme: a classic remains a classic; it stands all the tests of time and changing sensibilities; we read the classics not because we are required to do so, because we have been told to read them, but because they are wiser, more enduring, and provide more pleasure than lesser works. Cyril Connolly, in *Enemies of Promise*, comments that the true test of a writer is to write a book that can last ten years, not to write a best-seller. Most writers would agree.

Literature is news that STAYS news.

EZRA POUND
ABC OF READING (1934)

Sir, everything that is not literature is life.

JOSÉ SARAMAGO
THE HISTORY OF THE SIEGE OF LISBON (1996)

Definition of a classic: A book everyone is assumed to have read and often thinks they have.

ALAN BENNETT (1934–)

A classic is a book that has never finished saying what it has to say.

ITALO CALVINO (1923–1985)
THE LITERATURE MACHINE (1986)

Of course, literature is the only spiritual and humane career. Even painting tends to dumbness, and music turns people erotic, whereas the more you write the nicer you become.

VIRGINIA WOOLF (1882–1941)

To provoke dreams of terror in the slumber of prosperity has become the moral duty of literature.

ERNST FISCHER
ART AGAINST IDEOLOGY (1969)

The world must be all fucked up when men travel first-class and literature goes as freight.

GABRIEL GARCÍA MÁRQUEZ
ONE HUNDRED YEARS OF SOLITUDE (1967)

A classic is classic not because it conforms to certain structural rules, or fits certain definitions (of which its author had quite probably never heard). It is classic because of a certain eternal and irrepressible freshness.

EZRA POUND
ABC OF READING (1934)

How simple the writing of literature would be if it were only necessary to write in another way what has been well written. It is because we have had such great writers in the past that a writer is driven far out past where he can go, out to where no one can help him.

ERNEST HEMINGWAY
NOBEL PRIZE ACCEPTANCE SPEECH (1954)

Literature is mostly about having sex and not having children. Life is the other way around.

DAVID LODGE
THE BRITISH MUSEUM IS FALLING DOWN (1965)

Literature is the orchestration of platitudes.

THORNTON WILDER
IN *TIME* (JANUARY 12, 1953)

Literature transmits incontrovertible condensed experience . . . from generation to generation. In this way, literature becomes the living memory of a nation.

ALEXANDER SOLZHENITSYN
NOBEL PRIZE LECTURE (1970)

I hate everything that does not relate to literature; conversations bore me (even when they relate to literature), to visit people bores me, the joys and sorrows of my relatives bore me to my soul. Conversation takes the importance, the seriousness, the truth out of everything I think.

> FRANZ KAFKA (1883–1924)

What is so wonderful about great literature is that it transforms the man who reads it towards the condition of the man who wrote.

> E. M. FORSTER
> *TWO CHEERS FOR DEMOCRACY* (1951)

Literature is the human activity that takes the fullest and most precise account of variousness, possibility, complexity and difficulty.

> LIONEL TRILLING
> *THE LIBERAL IMAGINATION* (1950)

The land of literature is a fairy land to those who view it at a distance, but, like all other landscapes, the charm fades on a nearer approach, and thorns and briars become visible.

WASHINGTON IRVING (1783–1859)

The decline of literature indicates the decline of a nation.

JOHANN WOLFGANG VON GOETHE
IN JOHANN ECKERMANN, *CONVERSATIONS WITH GOETHE* (1836)

Governments are suspicious of literature because it is a force that eludes them.

ÉMILE ZOLA
LE ROMAN EXPÉRIMENTAL (1880)

It takes a great deal of history to produce a little literature.

HENRY JAMES
HAWTHORNE (1879)

The gem of all the characters, needless to say, is Falstaff . . . adorable rogue, man of fine and unconquerable spirit, peerless creation of the highest wit—any one of us would give ten years for the privilege of spending an hour with him.

GUISEPPE TOMASI DI LAMPEDUSA (1896–1957)

Classic—a book people praise and don't read.

MARK TWAIN
FOLLOWING THE EQUATOR (1897)

A great book should leave you with many experiences, and slightly exhausted at the end. You live several lives while reading it.

WILLIAM STYRON
WRITERS AT WORK—FIRST SERIES (1958)

When you re-read a classic you do not see more in the book than you did before; you see more in you than there was before.

CLIFTON FADIMAN
ANY NUMBER CAN PLAY (1957)

It is with literature as with law or empire—an established name is an estate in tenure or a throne in possession.

EDGAR ALLAN POE (1809–1849)

A classic is something that everybody wants to have read and nobody wants to read.

MARK TWAIN (1835–1910)

What a sense of security in an old book, which Time has criticized for us.

JAMES RUSSELL LOWELL (1819–1891)

The house of fiction has in short not one window, but a million—
a number of possible windows not to be reckoned rather; every
one of which has been pierced, or is still pierceable, in its vast
front, by the need of the individual vision and by the pressure of
the individual will.

HENRY JAMES
PREFACE TO *THE PORTRAIT OF A LADY* (1881)

Americans like fat books and thin women.

RUSSELL BAKER (1925–)

Great literature is simply language charged with meaning to the
utmost possible degree.

EZRA POUND
HOW TO READ (1931)

A truly great book should be read in youth, again in maturity, and once more in old age, as a fine building should be seen by morning light, at noon, and by moonlight.

ROBERTSON DAVIES (1913–1995)

THE ENTHUSIASMS OF ROBERTSON DAVIES

All modern American literature comes from one book by Mark Twain called *Huckleberry Finn* . . . American writing comes from that. There was nothing before. There has been nothing as good since.

ERNEST HEMINGWAY

GREEN HILLS OF AFRICA (1935)

The thing that teases the mind over and over for years, and at last gets itself put down rightly on paper—whether little or great, it belongs to Literature.

SARAH ORNE JEWETT (1849–1909)

Literature, the most seductive, the most deceiving, the most dangerous of professions.

JOHN MORLEY (1838–1923)

The newspaper is the natural enemy of the book, as the whore is of the decent woman.

GONCOURT BROTHERS
EDMOND DE GONCOURT (1822–1896)
JULES DE GONCOURT (1830–1870)

Every book is a failure.

GEORGE ORWELL (1903–1950)

Everywhere I go I'm asked if I think the university stifles writers. My opinion is that they don't stifle enough of them. There's many a best-seller that could have been prevented by a good teacher.

FLANNERY O'CONNOR (1925–1964)

Best-sellers are about murder, money, revenge, ambition, and sex, sex, sex. So are literary novels. But best-selling authors give you more per page: there are five murders, three world financial crises, two bankruptcies and a civil war in *A Dangerous Fortune*. There is more drama in it than a literary author will deal with in a lifetime of work.

KEN FOLLETT
IN BARRY TURNER, *THE WRITER'S COMPANION* (1996)

There are books of which the backs and covers are by far the best parts.

CHARLES DICKENS (1812–1870)

The body of literature, with its limits and edges, exists outside some people and inside others. Only after the writer lets literature shape her can she perhaps shape literature.

ANNIE DILLARD (1945–   )

I think we ought to read only the kind of books that wound and stab us.

FRANZ KAFKA (1883–1924)

Collecting Books

A Special Section by
Nicholas A. Basbanes

Most of the quotations in this section were drawn from
*A Gentle Madness: Bibliophiles, Bibliomanes, and the Eternal
Passion for Books*, by Nicholas A. Basbanes, Henry Holt,
1995, used with permission of the author.

Of what use are books without number and complete collections, if their owner barely finds time in the course of his life even to read their titles?

SENECA (4 B.C.–A.D. 65)

Books would be precious things indeed, if the mere possession of them guaranteed culture to their owners.

LUCIAN OF SAMOSATA (A.D. 115–180)

Maybe I have more than I need, but it is the same with books as with everything else—success in finding them spurs one on to greed for more.

PETRARCH (1304–1374)

No dearness of price ought to hinder a man from the buying of books, if he has the money that is demanded for them, unless it be to withstand the malice of the seller or to await a more favourable opportunity of buying.

RICHARD DE BURY, LORD CHANCELLOR OF ENGLAND,
   BISHOP OF DURHAM
PHILOBIBLON (1345)

In fact, the fame of our love of them had been soon winged abroad everywhere, and we were reported to burn with such desire for books, and especially old ones, that it was more easy for any man to gain our favour by means of books than of money.

BISHOP RICHARD DE BURY
PHILOBIBLON (1345)

What wild desires, what restless torments seize
The hapless man, who feels the book-disease . . .

DR. JOHN FERRIAR
"THE BIBLIOMANIA: AN EPISTLE TO RICHARD HEBER, ESQ."
POEM (1863)

It has raged chiefly in palaces, castles, halls, and gay mansions, and those things which in general are supposed not to be inimical to health, such as cleanliness, spaciousness, and splendour, are only so many inducements toward the introduction and propagation of the BIBLIOMANIA! What renders it particularly formidable is that it rages in all seasons of the year, and at all periods of human existence.

> REV. THOMAS FROGNALL DIBDIN
> *THE BIBLIOMANIA* (1809)

I am willing even to scrape a dunghill, if I may find a jewel at the bottom.

> REV. JEREMY BELKNAP (1744–1798)
> FOUNDER OF THE MASSACHUSETTS HISTORICAL SOCIETY

There is nothing like having a good repository, and keeping a lookout, not waiting at home for things to fall into the lap, but prowling about like a wolf for the prey.

> REV. JEREMY BELKNAP (1744–1798)

The bibliophile is the master of his books, the bibliomaniac their slave.

HANNS BOHATTA (1864–1947)

Books are my disease.

JAMES LOGAN (1674–1751)
IN EDWIN WOLF II, *THE LIBRARY OF JAMES LOGAN* (1974)

No gentleman can comfortably do without three copies of a book. One he must have for his show copy, and he will probably keep it in his country house. Another he will require for his own use and reference; and unless he is inclined to part with this, which is very inconvenient, or risk the injury of his best copy, he must have a third at the service of his friends.

RICHARD HEBER (1773–1833)
KEPT MORE THAN 200,000 BOOKS IN EIGHT HOUSES IN FIVE COUNTRIES

I looked round me with amazement. I had never seen rooms, cupboards, passages, and corridors, so choked, so suffocated with books . . . Up to the very ceilings the piles of volumes extended; while the floor was strewed with them, in loose and numerous heaps.

REV. THOMAS FROGNALL DIBDIN
FOLLOWING THE DEATH OF RICHARD HEBER, AND SEEING HIS LIBRARY
AT PIMLICO FOR THE FIRST TIME
REMINISCENCES OF A LITERARY LIFE (1836)

"And why," I asked myself, "why should I have learned that this precious book exists, if I am never to possess it—never even to see it? I would go to seek it in the burning heart of Africa, or in the icy regions of the Pole if I knew where it were there. But I do not know where it is. I do not know if it be guarded in a triple-locked iron case by some jealous bibliomaniac. I do not know if it be growing mouldy in the attic of some ignoramus. I shudder at the thought that perhaps its torn-out leaves may have been used to cover the pickle-jars of some housekeeper.

ANATOLE FRANCE
THE CRIME OF SYLVESTRE BONNARD (1881)

O my darling books! A day will come when you will be laid out on the salesroom table, and others will buy and possess you— persons, perhaps, less worthy of you than your old master. Yet how dear to me are they all! Have I not chosen them one by one, gathered them in with the sweat of my brow? I do love you all!

SILVESTRE DE SACY (1758–1838)

My wish is that my drawings, my prints, my curiosities, my books—in a word, these things of art which have been the joy of my life—shall not be consigned to the cold tomb of a museum, and subject to the stupid glance of the passer-by; but I require that they shall all be dispersed under the hammer of the Auctioneer, so that the pleasure which the acquiring of each one of them has given me shall be given again, in each case, to some inheritor of my own tastes.

EDMOND DE GONCOURT (1822–1896)
FROM HIS WILL

In nature the bird who gets up the earliest catches the most worms, but in book-collecting the prizes fall to birds who know worms when they see them.

MICHAEL SADLEIR
THE COLOPHON (NUMBER 3, 1930)

They may some day want to move my books, they may want to move my paintings, but they will think twice before they move me.

RUSH C. HAWKINS
ON THE MATTER OF HAVING HIMSELF BURIED WITH HIS COLLECTION
OF INCUNABULA IN PROVIDENCE, RHODE ISLAND (1903)

Anything can be anywhere.

LARRY MCMURTRY
CADILLAC JACK (1982)

Bibliophiles. An idiot class.

A. E. HOUSMAN (1859–1936)
IN JOHN CARTER, *TASTE AND TECHNIQUE IN BOOK COLLECTING* (1948)

I wish to have one copy of every book in the world.

SIR THOMAS PHILLIPPS (1792–1872)

IN A. N. L. MUNBY, *PORTRAIT OF AN OBSESSION* (1967)

I am booked out of one wing and ratted out of the other.

WIFE OF SIR THOMAS PHILLIPPS

IN A. N. L. MUNBY, *PORTRAIT OF AN OBSESSION* (1967)

If the great collections of the past had not been sold where would I have found my books.

ROBERT HOE III (1839–1909)

THE LIBRARY OF ROBERT HOE OF NEW YORK (VOL. I, 1911)

Fear [that I] cannot buy [the] Caxton [for] under forty thousand, and possibly not at this price. Shall I buy at any price?

BELLE DA COSTA GREENE (1879–1950)
IN A CABLE TO JOHN PIERPONT MORGAN

Use your discretion. Would give seventy-five or even a hundred rather than lose.

JOHN PIERPONT MORGAN (1837–1913)
IN REPLY TO BELLE DA COSTA GREENE

A great library cannot be constructed—it is the growth of ages.

JOHN HILL BURTON
THE BOOK-HUNTER (1862)

It is, as you observe, the general ambition of the class to find value where there seems to be none, and this develops a certain skill and subtlety, enabling the operator, in the midst of a heap of rubbish, to put his finger on those things which have in them the latent capacity to become valuable and curious.

> JOHN HILL BURTON
> *THE BOOK-HUNTER* (1862)

We wouldn't want to think that the president of one of our major companies would be the kind of man foolish enough to pay a hundred thousand dollars for a book!

> JOHN D. ROCKEFELLER (1839–1937)
> TO HENRY CLAY FOLGER
> IN EDWIN WOLF II AND JOHN FLEMING, *ROSENBACH* (1960)

I am not exaggerating when I say that to a true collector the acquisition of an old book is a rebirth.

> WALTER BENJAMIN (1892–1940)
> *ILLUMINATIONS: ESSAYS AND REFLECTIONS* (1969)

The trouble with you is that you're like every other God-damned collector.

ANONYMOUS BOOKSELLER TO ROBERT H. TAYLOR

I don't ask for any better tribute.

ROBERT H. TAYLOR TO BOOKSELLER

I was put on this earth to collect books, not to write them. It has taken me fifty years to gather my collection, now forever happily in residence at Bryn Mawr College, and I would like to add to its shelves from to time to time.

SEYMOUR ADELMAN
THE MOVING PAGEANT (1977)

If there is one thing that a book-collector loves more than acquiring books, it is talking about them. Indeed, there are scribes of good repute who maintain that bibliophiles prate so incessantly of their books that they have no time to read.

HARRY B. SMITH
THE SENTIMENTAL LIBRARY (1914)

If I were the owner of the copy of Keats's *Poems* which Shelley had in his pocket when he was drowned, and which Trelawney threw upon the funeral pyre, I confess I should never read it, though I might keep it in a little shrine and burn incense to it.

HARRY B. SMITH
THE SENTIMENTAL LIBRARY (1914)

"What shall I do with all my books?" was the question; and the answer, "Read them," sobered the questioner. But if you cannot read them, at any rate handle them and, as it were, fondle them. Peer into them. Let them fall open where they will . . . If they cannot enter the circle of your life, do not deny them at least a nod of recognition.

WINSTON CHURCHILL
THOUGHTS AND ADVENTURES (1932)

With thought, patience, and discrimination, book passion becomes the signature of a person's character. When out of control and indulged to excess, it lets loose a fury of bizarre behavior.

NICHOLAS A. BASBANES (1943–)

My copy of *Paradise Lost* once belonged to Deborah Milton Clarke, the daughter who took Milton's dictation after he went blind. For me, it was like the apostolic succession. I was touching the hand that touched the Hand.

REYNOLDS PRICE
IN AN INTERVIEW WITH NICHOLAS A. BASBANES

When the rulers of kingdoms today have crumbled into the dust and their names forgotten of the people, the memory of a maker of a great collection will be a household word in the mouths of thousands. This is the real road to fame.

HENRY E. HUNTINGTON (1850–1920)
AMERICAN BOOK COLLECTOR (MAY–JUNE 1973)

Buy good books, and read them; the best books are the commonest, and the last editions are always the best, if the editors are not blockheads, for they may profit from the former. But take care not to understand editions and title-pages too well. It always smells of pedantry, and always of learning.

THE EARL OF CHESTERFIELD (1694–1773)
IN A LETTER TO HIS SON PHILIP STANHOPE (MARCH 19, 1750)

Every man must die sooner or later, but good books must be preserved.

> DON VINCENTE
> SPANISH MONK CONVICTED AND EXECUTED IN 1836 FOR KILLING A MAN
> FOR A BOOK

It is paradoxical, but true, that not a single great library in the world has been formed by a great scholar.

> DR. A. S. W. ROSENBACH
> *BOOKS AND BIDDERS* (1927)

I have known men to hazard their fortunes, go long journeys halfway about the world, forget friendships, even lie, cheat, and steal, all for the gain of a book.

> DR. A. S. W. ROSENBACH
> *BOOKS AND BIDDERS* (1927)

Books were stacked under tables, piled up on beds, heaped in bundles on both sides of the stairways, pressed three and four deep in bookcases and onto ceiling-height shelving that lined every room and all hallways. Every room was awash with teetering piles of books, tied bundles of pamphlets, and stacks of magazines, so that we had to inch our way along trails that hacked into a bookman's jungle.

ROBERT VOSPER
ON ENTERING THE HOME OF A DECEASED BIBLIOMANIAC
PAPERS OF THE BIBLIOGRAPHICAL SOCIETY OF AMERICA 55 (3RD QUARTER, 1961)

I am still buying books. It is like getting pregnant after the menopause; it's not supposed to happen.

CHEF LOUIS SZATHMARY (1919–1996)
IN AN INTERVIEW WITH NICHOLAS A. BASBANES

You can never be too thin, too rich, or have too many books.

CARTER BURDEN (1941–1996)
VOGUE (MARCH 1987)

You ask is this an obsession? Yes. I'm sure this is an obsession. But is that bad? You have to be obsessive, I think, or it just doesn't work.

> DAVID KARPELIS
> IN AN INTERVIEW WITH NICHOLAS A. BASBANES

I used to read catalogues in bed at night, and I would say to my wife, "Look at this, here's a book I paid fifty dollars for, a dealer wants thirty-five hundred for it." And my wife would say, "So sell it." Well, today she finally got her wish.

> RAYMOND EPSTEIN
> ON THE DAY IN 1992 THAT HIS COLLECTION OF FIRST EDITIONS SOLD
> FOR MORE THAN $1 MILLION AT AUCTION

Some people are obsessed about collecting books; I collect book thieves. They are my obsession. I have hundreds of folders documenting cases of book theft, probably the most extensive file of its kind anywhere.

> WILLIAM A. MOFFETT (1932–1995)
> IN AN INTERVIEW WITH NICHOLAS A. BASBANES

Statistically, there has not been anyone who stole more books of such obviously high quality from more libraries than Stephen Blumberg.

WILLIAM A. MOFFETT (1932–1995)

Well, maybe that's a rationalization on my part. I was sort of— okay, let's put it this way: they were sort of on an interlibrary loan to me. That's what I figure.

STEPHEN C. BLUMBERG (1948–), BIBLIOKLEPTOMANIAC
IN AN INTERVIEW WITH NICHOLAS A. BASBANES

Most bibliophiles in our time . . . go to great lengths to preserve the virginal state of their darlings, their *mint* loveliness, enshrining them for protection and honour in rich cases bearing the *counterfeit presentment* of books.

HOLBROOK JACKSON
THE ANATOMY OF BIBLIOMANIA VOL. II (1931)

Book-love, I say again, lasts throughout life, it never flags or fails, but, like Beauty itself, is *a joy for ever*.

HOLBROOK JACKSON
THE ANATOMY OF BIBLIOMANIA VOL. II (1931)

Index

A

Addison, Joseph (1672–1719), 102

Adelman, Seymour, 221

Adler, Bill, 180

Adler, Mortimer J. (1902–   ), 138

Aeschylus (525–456 B.C.), 60

Albee, Edward F. (1928–   ), 41

Allen, Woody (1935–   ), 105

Amis, Martin (1949–   ), 56

Angelou, Maya (1928–   ), 36, 65,
   106, 107, 133

Appelfeld, Aharon (1932–   ), 65

Aristotle (384–322 B.C.), 35, 43

Arnold, Martin, 189

Atwood, Margaret (1939–   ), 42,
   48, 65, 180

Auden, W. H. (1907–1973), 17, 66

Austen, Jane (1775–1817), 35, 115

B

Babel, Isaac (1894–c. 1940), 32

Bacon, Francis (1561–1626), 11,
   14, 43, 96

Bagehot, Walter (1826–1877), 47,
   166

Baker, Russell (1925–   ), 203

Baldwin, James (1924–1987), 99

Balfour, Arthur James
   (1848–1930), 84

Barnes, Julian (1946–   ), 79, 110

Barrie, J. M. (1860–1937), 185,
   188

229

C

M

N

T

U